COOKING
IN
THE ORCHARD

Megan Mallory

Cover by John Cabalka

Designs by Maxwell Moray

Gala Books

2147 Laguna Canyon Road
Laguna Beach, California 92652

First Printing 1972
Library of Congress Catalog Number: 72-78043
ISBN Number: 0-912448-05-9
© Copyright 1972 by Gala Books
Composed and Printed in the United States of America

TABLE OF CONTENTS

A culinary tribute to the fruits of the orchard and their multiple uses in breads, casseroles, salads, entrees, soups, vegetables, stuffings, sauces, and desserts.

Worldly ways of cooking your favorite nuts in chicken and seafood dishes, Chinese stir-frys, breads, sauces, cereals, and vegetables.

Lively dishes seasoned with spices from the orchard. Recipes feature a variety of unusual foods using cinnamon, cloves, nutmeg, allspice, bay leaves, carob, and chocolate.

A side trip to the field kitchen with recipes for fruits of the field as well as peanuts and sunflower seeds. Chapter includes unique breads, soup, entrees, salads, preserves, and desserts.

THE FLOWERING KITCHEN

The flowering orchard is a celebration of life and good eating. It's a natural setting for the world's most beautiful kitchen.

The orchard yields a banquet of golden and scarlet fruits, rich avocados and olives, savory nut meats, and aromatic spices from every corner of the green earth. These ambrosial foods cook into homemade breads, casseroles, soups, sauces, desserts—everything you can imagine, and then some.

Orchard cooking is as natural as nature, and just as inventive. It blooms with freshly picked flavors from the zesty lemon to the subtle almond, the rich plum to the lively clove.

One of the greatest delights of this leafy kitchen is its versatility. Fruits, nuts, and spices have multiple talents that open up a world of original cooking. In this kitchen, cinnamon spices a chicken, grapefruit flavors a fish, and pistachios top a pilaf. The apple is more than a pie; it's also a super soup, an apple-and-cheese bread, a spicy cake, a souffle, and a casserole baked with chicken.

Orchard cooking is unique for its taste of honey as a natural sweetner. Honey is not only nutritious, but delicious! All ingredients in this nature kitchen are keyed to good flavor and good nutrition; the unprocessed raw sugar, whole wheat pastry flour, natural brown rice, whole grain cereals, and vegetable margarine.

In addition to the fruits of the bough, this book also includes a chapter on the fruits of the field and the vine. You're also offered a choice pick of recipes from berry breads to stuffed grape leaves.

Whatever the season, the orchard kitchen is always open. Most of the ingredients are available the year around. For those fruits that are seasonable, dried or canned fruit may be easily substituted.

Recipes in this book are for 4 people, but the portions are generous and can be stretched.

It is fitting that the orchard is the domain of Bacchus, God of the vine, bon vivant, and immortal gourmet.

FRUITFUL TIPS

There's nothing esoteric about buying good fruit. All you need is an educated eye and thumb, so commit these tips to your memory bank:

Apples should be firm with a good, bright color—whatever the variety. Make sure they're smooth and free of bruises that cause rapid spoiling. Big apples bake better than small; and green apples are best for cooking. There is no substantial proof that an apple a day keeps the psychiatrist away.

Peaches, apricots, plums, and pears are tastiest when they have an even, mellow color and are slightly soft to the touch. Avoid hard peaches with a green background since they seldom ripen later—no matter how you coax them with sunlamp treatments, or sunlit terraces.

The juiciest oranges, lemons, grapefruit and limes have firm, fine-textured, or fairly smooth skins. They're also comparatively heavy for their size, since they're loaded with juice.

With cantaloupes, look for a thick, slightly raised "netting" over the outside skin; and, no trace of a stem. There should be a pronounced cavity where the melon was pulled from the vine. This is a badge of merit and maturity. Ripe melons also have a lovely ripe aroma, so follow your nose!

It's fairly easy to tell a good Honeydew by its creamy white color which is sometimes pale yellow on the underside. Greenish white Honeydews are usually duds that rarely mature in time.

Contrary to the Loyal Order of Watermelon Thumpers, you can't judge a ripe melon by its thump. It's safer to pick a big, green melon with a yellowish underside that indicates ripeness.

With pineapples, the bigger the pineapple the better the buy. Also the choicest ones have fresh green leaves, and a good fragrance.

As for grapes, look for ones that are firmly attached to their stems and which are plump and bright in color.

Some fruit, like avocados or bananas—or even pears, if you like—can be bought green and ripened at home in room temperature, away from the light. (Incidentally, to test the ripeness of an avocado, stick a tooth-pick in the stem end. If it comes out easily, you've got Guacamole for dinner!)

To prolong freshness, store fruit in the refrigerator, but don't wash it until you're ready to use it. If there isn't room in the fridge for the fruit you buy in quantity, like apples and oranges, store them in a cool, dark place.

The following are a few fruitful cooking tips:

Peaches peel more easily if they're first plunged into hot water for 20 to 30 seconds, and then into ice water. The same thing applies to apples; they're easier to pare if you give 'em a quick dunk in hot water.

Green bananas, and slightly under-ripe pears, are best for baking and broiling.

If you blanch a lemon for 2 minutes in boiling water, and then allow it to cool slightly, it yields half-again as much juice. Also, if you want to freshen slightly shriveled lemons, immerse them in hot water for 30 minutes.

The final tip is a triumph of brains over brawn. The easiest way to crack a coconut shell, after you remove the coconut "milk" is to heat it in a 350 degree oven for 30 minutes.

CHAPTER 1

COOKING
IN
THE ORCHARD

You don't need a tree house to cook in the orchard—only a verdant imagination. These beautiful dishes cook in any kitchen whether it's built-in or far out.

This chapter serves up your favorite fruits with bushels of new ideas for cooking them. First, is the lively lemon, which is all things to all cooks.

9

Right On! Lemon Sauce

The tart, zesty lemon yields the liveliest seasoning in the orchard kitchen. Here it sparks a savory lemon sauce that's right on with any kind of fish or seafood—or anything else that likes a nip of lemon.

1/3 cup margarine
2 tsp Dijon mustard
Juice of 1 lemon
1/4 tsp salt
1/4 tsp nutmeg
1 Tbsp parsley, chopped
1 Tbsp chives, chopped
4 egg yolks

Melt margarine in the top of a double boiler over barely simmering water. Stir in mustard, lemon juice, salt, nutmeg, parsley, and chives.

Beat egg yolks until thick and lemon-colored. Gradually stir into double boiler beating continuously until sauce thickens. This is especially good spooned over poached salmon or halibut.

Cool Broccoli with Lemon Dressing

A tsp of lemon makes the vegetables go down—also salads, meats, soups, sauces, marinades. Spoon this lemony dressing over cooked, chilled green beans or asparagus, too.

2 lb fresh broccoli
1/2 tsp salt

Lemon Dressing

1/2 cup lemon juice
1/4 cup salad oil
1/2 tsp paprika
1 tsp sugar
1/2 tsp salt
1 clove garlic, minced
2 Tbsp green onions, finely chopped
Garnish: 2 hard-cooked eggs, chopped

Remove leaves from broccoli and tough part of stalks. Steam broccoli until crisp tender. Season with salt. Cool to room temperature.

In a bowl combine lemon juice, salad oil, paprika, sugar, salt, garlic, and green onions. If possible, let dressing stand for an hour to mingle flavors.

Just before serving, spoon dressing over broccoli, and garnish with hard-cooked eggs.

Lemon Yogurt Pound Cake

When you bake this zesty pound cake, think kindly on Christopher Columbus, who brought the lemon to the New World.

6 egg whites
1/4 tsp cream of tartar
2 cups raw sugar
1 cup margarine
6 egg yolks

1 Tbsp lemon peel, finely chopped
4 Tbsp lemon juice
3 cups whole wheat pastry flour, sifted
1 tsp baking soda
1/4 tsp salt
1 cup yogurt

Beat egg whites with cream of tartar until stiff. Gradually fold in 1/2 cup of sugar until egg whites are glossy.

In a bowl, cream margarine with remaining 1 1/2 cups of sugar. Beat in egg yolks, one at a time, until mixture is smooth. Stir in lemon peel and lemon juice.

Sift flour again with baking soda and salt. Gradually add flour and yogurt alternately to margarine-egg mixture, stirring well until batter is smooth.

Fold egg whites into batter and pour into buttered and floured 10-inch tube pan. Bake in a 350 degree oven for 1 hour, or until cake is cooked. Cool 10 minutes in pan before removing to wire rack for cooling.

California Orange Chicken

Someone once said that California is a great place to live—if you're an orange. The sweet, amiable orange sauces a beautiful chicken topped with orange sections.

1/4 cup margarine
2 large whole chicken breasts, skinned and boned
3 Tbsp whole wheat pastry flour
1/4 cup orange honey
1/2 tsp salt
1/2 tsp dry mustard
1/2 tsp cinnamon
2 cups orange juice
2 Tbsp orange peel, finely chopped
2 navel oranges, peeled

Melt margarine in a skillet and saute chicken breasts until golden brown. Remove chicken.

Stir flour, honey, salt, mustard, and cinnamon in skillet until it forms a smooth paste. Gradually add orange juice, and stir until mixture begins to simmer. Return chicken to skillet, cover and gently simmer chicken over low heat until chicken is tender in about 20 minutes.

Sprinkle orange peel over top of chicken. Remove membranes from oranges and divide into sections. Place sections over chicken. Cover skillet and cook 5 minutes longer.

Orange Pecan Bread

The natural sweetness of oranges and honey combine with pecans to make a bread that is pure orchard.

1 large navel orange
1/3 cup orange honey
1/2 cup margarine
1 1/2 tsp salt
1 package of fresh, active dry yeast
1 egg, beaten
1/2 cup pecans, chopped
2 1/2 cups whole wheat pastry flour

Peel orange and remove white membrane; section orange. Put rind and orange sections into a food chopper and turn on blender until orange is reduced to pulp and juice.

Combine pulp and juice in a saucepan with honey, margarine and salt. Bring to a simmer, and cool to lukewarm. Dissolve yeast in liquid and beat well. Add egg and pecans and continue stirring. Add sufficient flour (about 2 1/2 cups) to make a stiff dough.

Knead dough on a floured board for 5 minutes. Put into an oiled mixing bowl, cover, and let dough rise for about an hour until it has doubled in size. Knead dough again for a few minutes, and put it into a greased loaf pan. Cover and let dough rise again until it has doubled in size.

Bake in a 375 degree oven for 40 to 50 minutes, or until done.

Tangerine Yakitori

No one can squeeze more flavor out of a tangerine than the Japanese.
This is a variation on the classic Yakitori or skewered, broiled chicken.

    2 large whole chicken breasts, skinned and boned
1 bunch green onions
1/2 cup tangerine juice
2 Tbsp soy sauce
1/4 cup dry sherry
1 clove garlic, minced
1/4 tsp powdered ginger or 1/2 tsp fresh ginger root, shredded

Cut each breast into 4 pieces making 1-inch wide strips. Cut the white part of the onions into 1 1/4 inch pieces. Thread chicken and onions lengthwise, alternately on four skewers.

Mix together tangerine juice with soy sauce, sherry, garlic, and ginger. Brush chicken and onion with sauce. Broil over medium hot coals on a grill or hibachi; or place skewers 4 inches from broiler. Baste chicken frequently with sauce, and turn skewers to brown chicken on both sides. Test chicken in 8 to 10 minutes to see if it is cooked through.

To serve, roll up chicken pieces and skewer on Japanese style wooden skewers. Serve with steamed rice.

Grapefruit Cake

While the grapefruit tree may be sacred to weight-watchers, it also yields sweet temptations.

1 1/2 cups whole wheat
   pastry flour
3/4 cup raw sugar
1 1/2 tsp baking powder
1/2 tsp salt
1/4 cup water
1/4 cup vegetable oil
3 egg yolks, beaten
4 Tbsp grapefruit juice

1 tsp grated lemon rind
3 egg whites
1/4 tsp cream of tartar
grapefruit sections
2 8 oz packages cream cheese, softened
3 Tbsp lemon juice
1 Tbsp grated lemon rind
2/3 cup orange honey
2 Tbsp grapefruit pulp

Sift together flour, sugar, baking powder and salt. Stir in water, oil, egg yolks, grapefruit juice and lemon rind. Beat mixture until smooth.

Beat egg whites with cream of tartar until whites are stiff. Fold into cake batter until just blended. Pour into unbuttered cake pan and bake in a 350 degree oven for 30 minutes, or until cake is done.

Invert pan on wire rack and let cake cool.

To make frosting, beat together cream cheese, lemon juice, lemon rind, honey and grapefruit pulp.

Cut cake in half horizontally and spread with frosting on bottom half. Top with several grapefruit sections. Add second layer; frost top and sides and garnish with more grapefruit sections.

Baked Fish with Grapefruit?

Yes and it's delicious! The grapefruit adds just the right zing!

1/4 cup green onions, thinly sliced
4 Tbsp margarine
1 cup soft bread crumbs
1/2 tsp salt
1/4 tsp pepper
1/4 tsp allspice
1 grapefruit
4 salmon or halibut steaks
3 Tbsp margarine, melted
Garnish: chopped parsley

Saute onions in margarine until soft. Stir in bread crumbs, salt, pepper, and allspice.

Cut grapefruit lengthwise—removing sections from the rind and white membrane. Reserve grapefruit juice.

Place fish in a buttered casserole, and pour over grapefruit juice. Spoon seasoned breadcrumbs over top of fish.

Bake in a hot 450 degree oven for 10 minutes.

Place grapefruit sections over bread crumbs; spoon over melted margarine and continue baking in a 375 degree oven for another 15 minutes, or until fish is cooked and easily flakes. Baste fish frequently during baking.

Garnish with parsley before serving.

Spicy Apple Cake

The backyard apple orchard has borne generations of tree climbers and apple munchers. The apple remains man's favorite fruit. Bake it in a spicy nut cake with this Lemon Honey Frosting.

2 eggs, beaten
2 cups raw sugar
1 tsp vanilla
1/2 cup vegetable oil
2 cups whole wheat pastry flour
2 tsp baking soda

2 tsp baking powder
2 tsp cinnamon
3/4 tsp salt
1 cup walnuts, chopped
4 cups apples, peeled and
finely chopped

Beat together eggs, sugar, and vanilla. Stir in oil until smooth.

Sift together flour, baking soda, baking powder, cinnamon, and salt; gradually beat into egg-sugar mixture. Add nuts and apple; stir well.

Pour into a greased and floured 11 x 7-inch baking pan. Bake for 1 hour in a 325 degree oven.

LEMON HONEY FROSTING

In a bowl blend together 8 oz of softened cream cheese, 2 Tbsp margarine, 1/3 cup orange honey, 3 Tbsp lemon juice, 2 Tbsp grated lemon peel, 1 tsp vanilla, and 1/2 tsp salt. Chill briefly in refrigerator before spreading over cake.

Ms. Apple Chicken

Whether you're a Miss, Mrs. or Ms., this apple-flavored chicken is a tempting dish to serve your favorite male chauvinist pig.

1 Tbsp salt
1/2 tsp pepper
1/2 tsp paprika
1 cup whole wheat pastry flour
2 small frying chickens
  cut into serving pieces
6 Tbsp margarine
3 large green apples, peeled,
  cored, and quartered

3 Tbsp raw sugar
1 tsp ground ginger
1 tsp cinnamon
1 tsp allspice
salt to taste
1 1/2 cups white wine
1/2 cup apple cider
3 Tbsp whole wheat pastry flour
2 Tbsp water

Mix together salt, pepper, paprika, and flour. Dip chicken pieces in this seasoned flour, shaking off any excess.

Melt margarine in a skillet and quickly brown chicken. Transfer chicken to a casserole.

Add apples to skillet; sprinkle with sugar, and lightly brown.

Arrange apples in casserole around chicken. Season chicken and apples with ginger, cinnamon, and allspice, plus a little more salt to taste. Pour white wine and cider in the bottom of casserole, cover and bake in a 350 degree oven for 1 hour, or until chicken is tender.

Remove chicken and apples to a serving platter and keep warm.

Pour liquid into a skillet. Mix flour with water and stir into liquid. Simmer and stir until sauce thickens, then pour over chicken before serving.

Apple Onion Soup

Here's an oniony-tasting soup laced with the subtle flavor of apple. Sprinkle hot, homemade croutons on top just before serving.

3 Tbsp margarine
1/2 cup celery, diced
1 1/2 medium-sized onions, thinly sliced
1 carrot, thinly sliced
3 apples
4 cups beef bouillon
1 bay leaf
2 cups French bread, diced into croutons
4 Tbsp margarine

Melt margarine in saucepan, and saute celery, onion, and carrots for a few minutes.

Slice and core apples, but do not peel. Add apples to saucepan, and saute with vegetables for 7 or 8 minutes.

Pour beef bouillon into saucepan, and add bay leaf. Simmer soup until ingredients are very soft.

Put vegetables and apples through a sieve then return to soup.

Reheat soup and pour into bowls.

Saute diced French bread in margarine until golden brown and crisp. Sprinkle croutons over soup.

Apple Souffle

This is the only souffle in the world you can munch.

1/2 cup margarine
1/2 cup whole wheat pastry flour
2 cups milk
1/2 tsp salt
1/2 tsp cinnamon
6 Tbsp raw sugar
2 Tbsp lemon rind, grated
4 egg yolks
2 large apples, peeled
4 egg whites
3 Tbsp blanched, slivered almonds, toasted
Garnish: sour cream

Melt margarine and stir in flour. Gradually add milk and stir until smooth and thick. Season with salt, cinnamon, sugar, and lemon rind. Cool to lukewarm, and beat in egg yolks.

Cut each apple into 10 wedges. Remove core and seeds. Place apple slices over the bottom of a greased, straight-sided casserole or souffle dish.

Beat egg whites until stiff. Fold whites into milk-flour mixture. Pour over apples, and sprinkle with almonds.

Place casserole in a pan of hot water, and bake in a 325 degree oven for 1 hour and 15 minutes, or until top is light-brown and firm.

Serve with a side dish of sour cream.

Apple Cheddar Bread

Apples and Cheddar have a natural affinity. No wonder they make a harmonious bread.

1/2 cup margarine
3/4 cup raw sugar
2 eggs, beaten
1 3/4 cup whole wheat pastry flour
1 tsp baking powder
1/2 tsp baking soda
1/2 tsp salt
1/2 tsp ginger
1 tsp cinnamon
1 cup unpeeled apples, cored and finely chopped
3/4 cup sharp Cheddar cheese, grated
1/2 cup pecans, chopped
4 Tbsp wheat germ

Cream margarine and sugar together. Beat in eggs until well blended.

Sift together flour, baking powder, baking soda, salt, ginger, and cinnamon. Stir 1/3 of the flour mixture into the egg-sugar mixture, and beat well. Add apples, cheese, and pecans; and stir in the remaining flour and wheat germ.

Pour batter into a greased loaf pan, and bake in a 350 degree oven for 1 hour, or until done. Cool before removing from pan.

You'll flip over this upside down, down-side up, apple pie. The bottom, which becomes the top, is covered with pecans.

4 Tbsp margarine
1/2 cup pecan halves
1/2 cup raw sugar
1 Tbsp molasses
Pie crust pastry for double-crust 9-inch pie
5 large apples, peeled, cored and sliced
2 Tbsp lemon juice
1/2 cup raw sugar
1 Tbsp whole wheat pastry flour
1/2 tsp cinnamon
1/2 tsp nutmeg
1/4 tsp salt

Spread margarine evenly on bottom and sides of pie pan. Press pecan halves around the sides and bottom of pan.

Mix sugar and molasses together and pat sugar evenly over pecans.

Divide pastry dough in half, and roll out the bottom crust. Fit crust inside teflon pie pan covering sides and bottom.

Sprinkle apples with lemon juice and combine with sugar, flour, cinnamon, nutmeg, and salt. Spread apple mixture in pie pan over pastry. Cover with a second crust; and prick top with a fork.

Bake pie in a 400 degree oven for 50 minutes, or until done. Cool and invert pie with the pecan bottom on top.

The exotic persimmon, apple of the orient, makes a great down home pudding.

1 cup raw sugar
1 cup whole wheat pastry flour, sifted
1 Tbsp baking soda
1/2 tsp cinnamon
1/2 tsp nutmeg
1/2 tsp ginger
1/2 cup milk
1 tsp vanilla
1 Tbsp melted margarine
1/2 cup chopped walnuts
1/2 cup raisins
1 cup persimmon pulp

Mix together sugar, flour, soda, cinnamon, nutmeg, and ginger. Stir in milk, and beat well. Add vanilla and margarine. Stir in walnuts, raisins, and persimmon pulp. Mix thoroughly.

Pour into greased baking dish, cover, and set in a pan of water. Bake 1 hour, to 1 hour and 15 minutes, in a 375 degree oven.

Serve hot or cold with the following Lemon Sauce: In the top of a double boiler stir together 1 cup raw sugar with the juice of 1 lemon, 1 Tbsp grated lemon rind, 1 beaten egg, 1/3 cup margarine, and 4 Tbsp water. Stir and simmer sauce until it thickens.

Persimmon Cookies

Persimmons also translate into an All-American cookie.

2 cups whole wheat pastry flour
1 tsp baking soda
1/4 tsp salt
1 tsp cinnamon
1/2 tsp nutmeg
1/2 tsp cloves
1/2 cup margarine
1 cup raw sugar
1 tsp grated lemon or orange rind
1 large egg, beaten
1 tsp vanilla
1 cup persimmon pulp
1 cup walnuts, finely chopped
1/2 cup raisins

Sift together flour, baking soda, salt, cinnamon, nutmeg, and cloves.

Cream margarine with sugar until blended. Stir in lemon or orange rind, egg, vanilla, and persimmon pulp. Blend well and add flour mixture with walnuts and raisins.

Stir batter and drop dough by spoonfuls onto greased cookie sheet.

Bake cookies in a 350 degree oven for 20 minutes, or until done. Cool cookies on wire racks.

Baked Lima Beans & Pears

In ancient times the pear tree was worshipped as a protector of cattle. On special feast days it was decorated with candles, strung with cheeses, and heralded in song & dance. Here's another tasty tribute to the pear.

1 lb medium-sized dried lima beans
6 cups chicken broth
1/2 cup margarine, melted
3 fresh, cooked pears, peeled and cored
1/3 cup raw sugar
1 Tbsp molasses

Put lima beans in a pot with water to cover. Bring to a boil, and boil 2 minutes. Remove pot from heat, and let beans stand 1 hour. Drain. Return beans to pot, and pour in chicken broth. Cover and simmer beans until tender. Drain.

Cover the bottom of a casserole with 1/4 cup of melted margarine and spoon out a layer of beans.

Chop cooked pears finely and spread half the pears over the beans.

Mix sugar with molasses and sprinkle half the sugar over the pears. Repeat layers, ending with a layer of beans. Pour remaining margarine over the top of casserole.

Cover and bake in a 275 degree oven for 2 hours.

Baked Sesame Pear

The next best thing to a partridge in a pear tree is a chicken served with this savory baked pear.

   4 pears, peeled
2 Tbsp lemon juice
2 Tbsp raw sugar
1/2 cup breadcrumbs
3 Tbsp margarine, melted
3 Tbsp sesame seeds

Halve and core pears. Brush with lemon juice, and sprinkle with sugar. Place on baking sheet and broil 8 minutes, or until tender.

Combine crumbs, margarine and sesame seeds. Sprinkle on pears, and broil another 2 or 3 minutes until brown.

As a variation, try broiled pears with a topping of Cheddar cheese—instead of the crumb-sesame seed mixture. Broil cooked pears until cheese melts.

Pear Squares

The only square thing about this hep dessert is its shape.

4 large Anjou pears, peeled and cored
2 eggs, beaten
4 Tbsp whole wheat pastry flour
1/2 tsp salt
1 cup raw sugar
2 tsp vanilla
2 tsp baking powder
1 cup chopped walnuts

Slice pears and put them in a greased 8 x 8-inch baking pan.

Beat together eggs, flour, salt, sugar, vanilla, and baking powder. Stir in nuts. Pour batter over pears.

Bake for 35 minutes in a 350 degree oven. Cut into squares and serve warm.

Poached Pears in Orange Sauce

Pears are a fruit for all seasons—and reasons. Savor them as a dessert poached in a delicate orange-honey sauce.

1 1/2 cups fresh orange juice
2 Tbsp lemon juice
1/2 cup orange honey
3 Tbsp grated orange rind
4 pears, peeled, halved and cored

In a saucepan combine orange juice, lemon juice, honey, and orange rind. Bring to a simmer and add pears. Cover and gently poach pears for 15 minutes, or until tender. Turn pears several times while cooking.

Remove pears from pan; simmer sauce a few minutes longer. Pour sauce over pears and chill before serving.

Butterfly Shrimp with Apricot Sauce

The modest apricot has many talents. It's a sauce to shrimp, a flavor to bread, a stuff for stuffing, and a fruit for fruit butter. Try them all!

1 1/2 lbs large shrimp
2 eggs, beaten
1/2 cup water
3/4 cup whole wheat pastry flour, sifted

2 Tbsp cornstarch
1 tsp baking powder
1 tsp salt
1 Tbsp vegetable oil
1 qt vegetable oil

APRICOT SAUCE
1/4 cup pineapple juice
2 Tbsp dry mustard
2 Tbsp soy sauce

1 cup apricot jam
1 Tbsp grated lemon peel
1/4 cup lemon juice

Shell and devein shrimp, but leave on shrimp tails. Rinse shrimp in cold water.

Mix together a batter of eggs, water, flour, cornstarch, baking powder, salt, and 1 Tbsp vegetable oil.

Heat 1 qt vegetable oil in large skillet until oil reaches frying temperature, or 375 degrees. Dip shrimp into batter, then fry for 2 minutes on each side until golden brown. Drain shrimp on paper towels.

Combine pineapple juice, mustard, soy sauce, apricot jam, lemon peel, and lemon juice; beat well. Heat sauce in a skillet. Pour sauce into 4 individual small bowls for dipping the shrimp. Serve shrimp on a platter with boiled rice.

Unstuffy Stuffing

Here the delicate apricot flavors a brown rice stuffing. It's a lovely way of cooking your goose—or any fowl.

2 cups cooked cold brown rice
1 cup cooked dried apricots, chopped
1/2 cup celery stalks and leaves, chopped
3 Tbsp parsley, chopped
4 Tbsp onion, finely chopped and sauteed
3 Tbsp chives, chopped
1/8 tsp thyme
1/8 tsp mace
1/4 tsp nutmeg
1/8 tsp cloves
1/2 tsp salt
1/4 tsp pepper
1/4 cup margarine, melted

Combine all ingredients in a bowl and blend well. This makes approximately 4 cups of stuffing for a chicken, duck or turkey.

32 Apricot Nut Bread

Of all the fruit breads, this is the pick of the orchard!

1/2 cup raw sugar
2 Tbsp margarine
1 large egg, beaten
1 cup sour cream
1/4 cup milk
1 cup bran
1/2 cup diced pecans or walnuts
1 cup cooked dried apricots, drained
2 cups whole wheat pastry flour
4 tsp baking powder
1/2 tsp baking soda
1/2 tsp salt
1 Tbsp grated orange rind

Cream sugar and margarine. Beat in egg, sour cream, and milk. Stir in bran, pecans, or walnuts, and apricots.

Sift together flour, baking powder, soda, and salt. Blend these dry ingredients with sour cream-apricot mixture.

Pour batter into a greased 9-inch loaf pan, and let stand for 15 minutes. Bake for 1 hour in a 350 degree oven, or until bread is done.

Cool bread 10 minutes in pan before removing to a wire rack. Cool bread completely before slicing.

Apricot Butter

Apricot fruit butter is all fruit and no butter. The texture is smoother than jam, and the flavor is less sweet. Slather this tasty spread on toast or sandwiches, or spoon a generous dollop over ice cream.

3 lbs apricots
1 cup orange juice or pineapple juice
2 cups raw sugar
3/4 tsp nutmeg
juice of 1 lemon
1 tsp cinnamon
1/2 tsp allspice

Peel and pit apricots. Mash apricots to a pulp and pour pulp into a saucepan with orange juice, or pineapple juice. Simmer over a very low heat, stirring frequently until fruit is tender.

Put pulp through a sieve. Season with sugar, nutmeg, lemon juice, cinnamon, and allspice. Spoon mixture into a baking dish, and bake in a slow, 300 degree oven for 45 minutes to 1 hour, or until "butter" is thick enough to cling to the edge of the spoon. Ladle "butter" into hot sterlized mason jars, and seal. Makes approximately 2 qts.

Peach trees flower on Chinese scrolls and Persian paintings. Try the picturesque peach baked with chicken in a spicy orange sauce.

2 frying chickens, cut in serving pieces
1 tsp salt
1/2 tsp pepper
1 cup fresh orange juice
4 Tbsp Dijon mustard
1/4 cup orange honey
1/4 cup margarine, melted
1 clove garlic, crushed
1 Tbsp soy sauce
3 Tbsp dry sherry
1/2 tsp ginger
4 fresh peaches, peeled, halved, and pitted

Place chicken pieces in a shallow baking pan, and season with salt and pepper.

Bake, uncovered, in a 350 degree oven for 30 minutes.

In a bowl combine orange juice, mustard, honey, margarine, garlic, soy sauce, sherry, and ginger. Baste chicken with orange-honey sauce, and bake another 30 minutes, basting frequently.

Arrange peach halves around chicken. Baste with sauce; and continue baking another 15 minutes, or until chicken is tender.

Nature is the best cook. Sample her fruits straight from the orchard and field.

4 beautiful golden peaches
16 large, plump, ripe strawberries
1 cup fresh, pureed raspberries
4 Tbsp blanched, slivered almonds, toasted

Peel and pit peaches. Put 1 whole peach into each of 4 goblet glasses or cups. Add 4 strawberries to each glass, and spoon over 1/4 cup of pureed raspberries. Garnish with almonds.

The only sugar in this dish is the natural sugar of the fruits. Be sure the fruit is at the peak of perfection—ripe and fragrant.

The Peach Thing

This airy concoction looks like a fallen souffle; but don't panic, it's delicious with fresh peaches and a dab of sour cream. Have it for breakfast.

> 3 eggs, well beaten
> 1/2 cup milk
> 1/2 cup whole wheat pastry flour, sifted
> 1/2 tsp salt
> 2 Tbsp margarine, melted
> 1 Tbsp lemon juice
> 2 cups fresh peaches, peeled and sliced
> 3 Tbsp raw sugar
> Garnish: sour cream and cinnamon

Preheat oven to 450 degrees.

In a bowl beat together eggs, milk, flour, and salt until batter is smooth. Melt margarine in a 9-inch skillet with oven-proof handle, or round 9-inch baking dish, and pour in batter.

Bake on lower shelf of a preheated 450 degree oven for 15 minutes. Prick mixture with a fork in several places to collapse some of the puffiness. Reduce heat to 350 degrees and continue baking for another 10 minutes until "pancake" is golden brown on top.

Remove "pancake" from pan and drizzle with lemon juice.

Spoon peaches, which have been sweetened with sugar, over the top. Garnish with sour cream flavored with a touch of cinnamon.

Spanish Sangria

The Spanish drink their peaches. This Sangria from Cordoba is sparked with a fat, sliced peach and other aromatic fruits. Salud!

1 orange, thinly sliced and seeded
1 lemon, thinly sliced and seeded
1/2 cup fresh strawberries
1/2 cup fresh raspberries
1 peach, peeled and sliced
2 tsp raw sugar
1 oz Cointreau
1 oz brandy
1 bottle full-bodied red wine

Put orange and lemon slices in a pottery pitcher with strawberries, raspberries, and the sliced peach. Sprinkle with sugar and pour over the Cointreau and brandy. Let mixture stand for several hours.

Pour wine into pitcher with lots of ice cubes. Stir Sangria until it is completely chilled. Serve in chilled glasses.

Fresh Plum Tart

God must have loved plums. He made 2,000 varieties. Here's a recipe for the European purple plum in a great old-country tart.

2 cups whole wheat pastry flour
1 tsp baking powder
1/2 tsp salt
2 Tbsp raw sugar
1/2 cup margarine
2 lbs fresh purple plums, halved and pitted
3/4 cup raw sugar
1 tsp cinnamon
2 egg yolks, beaten
1 cup sour cream

Sift together flour, baking powder, salt, and sugar. Work margarine into flour mixture with a pastry blender until flour looks mealy.

With your hands pat an even layer of pastry over the bottom and halfway up the sides of an 8-inch, buttered baking pan. Press pastry against pan until it holds firmly.

Arrange plums over pastry shell, cavity side down.

Mix sugar with cinnamon, and sprinkle over plums.

Bake cobbler in a preheated 400 degree oven for 15 minutes.

Beat egg yolks with sour cream and spoon over the top of cobbler.

Bake another 30 minutes. Cut into squares and serve.

Plum Chutney Chicken

The prolific plum also simmers into a fabulous chutney. Served as a condiment with curries, or baked with chicken, this chutney is plum good.

2 lbs plums, pitted and quartered
1 lb green apples, peeled
   and cored
1 large onion, chopped
2 cups golden raisins
2 cups cider vinegar
2/3 cup raw sugar
1 Tbsp molasses
1 Tbsp salt
1 tsp ginger

1 tsp allspice
1/4 tsp each: cloves and
   dry mustard
1/4 tsp each: cayenne
   and nutmeg
2 frying chickens, cut into
   serving pieces
1/4 cup margarine
1 tsp salt

In a large saucepan combine plums, apples, onion, raisins, vinegar, sugar, molasses, salt, ginger, allspice, cloves, mustard, cayenne, and nutmeg. Bring to a boil, cover pan; and simmer about 1 1/2 hours over low heat, stirring frequently, until chutney is cooked and thick.

Reserve 1 cup of chutney for chicken; spoon remaining chutney into sterilized mason jars, and seal.

Lightly brown chicken in margarine. Place chicken in a single layer in a shallow baking pan. Season with salt. Cover and bake 45 minutes. Spoon 1 cup chutney over chicken and continue baking another 30 minutes or until chicken is tender.

Papaya Nut Bread

Shake a papaya tree and you have the basic ingredient for a fabulous fruit bread. If you're fresh out of papaya, you can substitute peaches.

2 1/2 cups whole wheat pastry flour
1 Tbsp baking powder
1/2 tsp salt
1/4 tsp nutmeg
1/4 tsp cinnamon
1/4 cup margarine
1/2 cup raw sugar
2 large eggs, beaten
2 Tbsp grated orange rind
2/3 cup milk
2 Tbsp whole wheat pastry flour
1/2 papaya, peeled and diced
1/2 cup walnuts, chopped

Sift together flour, baking powder, salt, nutmeg, and cinnamon.

Cream margarine with sugar, and beat in eggs and orange rind. Add dry ingredients to sugar-egg mixture, alternately, with milk. Beat batter until smooth.

Mix flour through papaya and walnuts, and add to batter.

Pour batter into a greased loaf pan; and bake in a 350 degree oven for 1 hour, or until done.

Cool in pan for 10 minutes before turning out on wire rack. Cool thoroughly.

Papaya Platter

*In the tropics you can pick this dinner yourself. The yogurt dressing is a
perfect accent for the fruit.*

1 1/2 cups yogurt
1/4 cup honey
1 Tbsp grated lemon peel
1/2 tsp nutmeg
1 large ripe papaya, peeled, seeded, and sliced
8 spears of fresh pineapple
2 cups of whole, hulled strawberries
4 bananas, peeled, and sliced lengthwise

In a bowl, mix together yogurt, honey, lemon peel, and nutmeg.
Refrigerate at least an hour to permit flavors to blend.

Prepare fruit the last minute before serving; and arrange papaya,
pineapple, strawberries, and bananas on a large platter.

Spoon over Yogurt Sauce.

Chicken with Cherries

Summer's sweet cherries add color and zest to a fruitful chicken.

2 small frying chickens cut into serving pieces
1 cup whole wheat pastry flour
1 Tbsp salt
1 tsp paprika
2 tsp curry powder
1/4 cup vegetable oil
2 cups dry white wine
1 large navel orange, peeled and sectioned
1 cup fresh Bing cherries, pitted
8 fresh pineapple spears
Garnish: avocado slices

Dip chicken pieces in flour which has been seasoned with salt, paprika and curry powder.

Heat oil in skillet and lightly brown chicken on all sides.

Remove chicken to casserole, pour in white wine, cover and bake chicken in a 350 degree oven for 45 minutes.

Arrange orange segments, cherries and pineapple spears over chicken and continue baking casserole for another 20 minutes or until fruit and chicken are tender.

Serve chicken on a large platter topped with fruit and garnished with avocado slices.

Redcoats' Cherry Sauce

This isn't a sauce to serve at a party for the Daughters of the American Revolution; but it's a fine old English way of saucing a duck, chicken, or game hen.

1 cup beef bouillon
1/2 cup currant jelly
1/2 cup port wine
1 1/2 Tbsp lemon juice
2 Tbsp orange rind, grated
1/2 cup red cherries, pitted

In a saucepan combine bouillon, jelly, wine, lemon juice, orange rind. Simmer, covered, for 10 minutes. Add cherries, and simmer another 5 minutes.

Fig Apples

The fig tree shared the Garden of Eden with the apple tree. It's not surprising they make a tempting twosome.

4 large red apples
6 Tbsp raw sugar
4 tsp chopped orange peel
1/3 cup dried figs, chopped
1/4 cup pitted dates, chopped
1/4 cup walnuts, chopped
1 tsp cinnamon
1/2 tsp ground cloves
2 Tbsp rum
4 Tbsp margarine
1 tsp cinnamon

Core apples and cut bottoms flat for a base. Pare apples down 1/4 of the way from the stem and place apples in a greased casserole. Make sure they do not touch each other.

Mix together sugar, orange peel, figs, dates, walnuts, cinnamon, and cloves. Moisten mixture with rum or water. Spoon mixture into apple cavities. Dot each apple with a liberal 1 Tbsp of margarine and dust with cinnamon. Pour 1/4 cup of water in the bottom of casserole.

Cover and bake in a 375 degree oven for 45 minutes, or until apples are cooked but still firm.

Italian Fig Salad

The sacred fig tree of Romulus, which grew in the Roman Forum, was revered by the Romans as a symbol of power. Have the divine fruit in an insalata Italiana.

2 large golden peaches, peeled and pitted
4 apricots, peeled and pitted
4 plums, pitted and peeled
4 figs, peeled
1/3 cup lemon juice
1/3 cup sugar

Cut peaches, apricots, plums, and figs into small chunks.

Mix lemon juice and sugar together, and pour over fruit. Toss well. Chill.

We recommend making this salad in the morning to serve in the evening.

Honey Date Cake

If cakes grew on trees, they'd taste like this.

2 cups whole wheat pastry flour
1 tsp salt
1 tsp baking soda
1 cup margarine
1 cup honey
2 eggs, well beaten
1/2 cup pitted dates, finely chopped

WALNUT FROSTING

8 oz cream cheese
1/3 cup honey
1/3 cup walnuts, finely chopped

Sift together flour, salt, and baking soda.

Cream margarine. Beat honey and eggs together. Gradually add honey mixture and dry ingredients, alternately, to margarine. Stir well.

Pour batter into a greased and floured 9-inch square baking pan. Bake for 25 to 30 minutes in a 350 degree oven until cake is done. Cool.

In a bowl beat together cream cheese, honey, and walnuts until mixture is creamy. Spread over top of cake.

Arabian Date Pilaf

While today oil sheiks gallop into the sunset in Rolls Royces, they still make their pilaf the ancient way—with dates and aromatic spices. Praise Allah!

3 Tbsp vegetable oil
1 1/2 cups brown rice
1/2 onion, finely chopped
1 tsp salt
3 3/4 cups water
1/4 tsp allspice
1/4 tsp cardamon
1/4 tsp cinnamon
1/4 tsp ground cloves
2 Tbsp margarine
1/8 cup blanched almonds, coarsely chopped
1/8 cup shelled pistachio nuts, coarsely chopped
1/3 cup golden raisins
1/2 cup pitted dates, coarsely chopped

Heat oil in a saucepan, and stir in rice until grains are coated with oil. Add onion, and saute for a few minutes until onion is soft. Pour in water; cover, and simmer for 30 minutes.

Add allspice, cardamon, cinnamon, and cloves. Continue simmering rice until cooked in 15 or 20 minutes.

Melt margarine in skillet and saute almonds, pistachio nuts, raisins, and dates until hot. Stir into rice before serving.

Mango Jam

In India, when the mango tree reaches maturity, it is married with great pomp and ceremony to a nearby jasmine or tammarind tree. A happily married tree produces better mangoes—and better mango jam.

2 large green mangoes, peeled
3 cups raw sugar
1/4 cup lime juice

Choose mangoes that are not fully ripened, still a bit green. Chop fruit coarsely to make approximately 4 cups of pulp.

Pour pulp into a saucepan, and stir in sugar and lime juice.

Simmer slowly for 1 hour, or until jam becomes thick. Stir frequently so the jam doesn't burn. It's best to place your saucepan on an asbestos pad to insure a low, even heat.

Spoon jam into hot, sterilized mason jars and seal.

Chicken with Sauteed Mangoes

The mango, lightly spiced and sauteed, shares a plate with a tropical chicken.

1/2 cup vegetable oil
1/2 cup fresh lime juice
3 Tbsp chives, chopped
1/2 tsp salt
1/2 tsp Tabasco Sauce
2 small broiler chickens, halved
1 large mango
2 Tbsp margarine
2 Tbsp raw sugar
4 whole cloves

Combine oil, lime, chives, salt, and Tabasco Sauce; brush liberally over chicken. Broil or grill chickens until golden brown and tender, basting frequently.

Peel and slice mango. Melt margarine in a skillet and stir in sugar and cloves. Add sliced mango sauteeing gently for 2 or 3 minutes until fruit is hot. Serve with chicken.

Tahiti Fish with Bananas

All you need to live in paradise is a Master Charge credit card—and a taste for baked bananas. This banana-orange fish is an island treat.

1 large navel orange, peeled and thinly sliced
2 Tbsp raw sugar
4 bananas
3 Tbsp lemon juice
whole wheat pastry flour
4 Tbsp margarine
4 filets of sole
1/2 tsp salt
4 Tbsp margarine
3 Tbsp lemon juice

Sprinkle orange slices with sugar.

Peel bananas and cut in halves lengthwise. Sprinkle with lemon juice, and leave 5 minutes.

Dip bananas in flour and saute in margarine until lightly browned. Remove from pan.

Season filet of sole with salt. Heat margarine in skillet and saute fish on both sides until lightly browned and cooked. Squeeze lemon juice over filets.

Arrange fish filets on a shallow baking dish. Place orange slices and bananas over fish. Heat remaining juices in skillet and pour over top.

Run dish under the broiler for 1 or 2 minutes to glaze top.

Banana Nut Bread

Some people go ape over this banana bread. Others merely love it.

2 1/2 cups whole wheat pastry flour
3 tsp baking powder
1/2 tsp salt
1 cup raw sugar
1/4 cup margarine
1 egg, beaten
1 cup mashed ripe bananas
2 Tbsp grated orange peel
1/2 cup milk
1 cup walnuts, coarsely chopped

Sift together flour, baking powder, and salt.

Beat together sugar, margarine, and egg until smooth. Add bananas, orange peel, and milk, mixing well. Gradually add flour mixture, and beat until smooth. Stir in nuts.

Pour into greased loaf pan and bake in a 350 degree oven for 1 hour, or until done.

Cool 10 minutes before removing from pan. Cool completely before cutting.

The first guacamole was stirred up by an Aztec priest. He discovered the versatile avocado makes a great party dip when having a few friends over for a ritual or rain dance.

2 very ripe avocados
1 tomato, peeled, seeded, and chopped
2 Tbsp lime juice
3 Tbsp green onions, finely chopped
1 Tbsp cilantro, finely minced or 1/2 tsp coriander
2 tsp canned green chilies, seeds removed
Tabasco sauce to taste
salt to taste

Peel and pit avocados, then mash with a fork. Stir in chopped tomato, lime juice, green onions, fresh cilantro (Chinese parsley) or coriander, green chilies, Tabasco, and salt to taste.

There are tasty ways of using guacamole other than the classic dip: Try a few dollops of guacamole on top of tomato, or carrot, soup—or jellied consomme. Build yourself a zesty salad by scooping out a fat tomato and filling it with guacamole and a topping of crisp, crumbled bacon. Garnish omelets and scrambled eggs with this lively sauce; or serve it with broiled steak, or chicken, for a piquant flavor. Guacamole also makes an original dip for cold, cooked artichokes.

Curried Shrimp in Avocado Shell

Here's seafood on the half shell—curried shrimps served in avocado halves.

2 Tbsp margarine
1 1/2 tsp curry powder
1 tsp salt
1 tomato, peeled and chopped
2 green onions, thinly sliced
2 Tbsp lime or lemon juice
1 cup sour cream
1 1/2 cups cooked small shrimp, peeled and deveined
4 avocados, halved

Melt margarine in a saucepan and stir in curry powder and salt. Add tomato and green onions, and saute until vegetables are soft. Stir in lime or lemon juice, sour cream, and cooked shrimp.

Simmer just enough to heat sauce and shrimp. Do not boil.

Peel and pit avocados and fill centers with hot curried shrimp.

Serve with brown rice and a dollop of chutney.

Stuffed Avocado with Chicken & Rice

Another dinner on the half shell—this time chicken and brown rice topped with a Cheddar cheese sour cream sauce.

3 Tbsp green onion, finely chopped
3 Tbsp green pepper, finely chopped
2 Tbsp margarine
1 cup cooked, boned chicken, cut into small chunks
1/2 cup cooked brown rice
4 avocados, halved
1 cup Cheddar cheese, grated
2 Tbsp margarine
1/2 cup sour cream

Saute green onions and green pepper in margarine until soft. Add chicken & brown rice, and stir briefly to heat. Peel and pit avocados; spoon rice-chicken filling into avocado cavities.

In the top of a double boiler melt cheese and margarine; beat in sour cream until sauce is creamy. Spoon sauce over avocados before serving.

Mexican Gazpacho Soup

A classic Spanish soup takes on the Mexican avocado.

3 hard-cooked eggs
2 Tbsp olive oil
1 garlic clove, crushed
1 1/2 tsp Worchestershire sauce
1 tsp dry mustard
2 shakes Tabasco sauce
Juice of 1 lemon
1 1/2 qts tomato juice
1 cucumber, peeled and thinly sliced
1 avocado, pitted, peeled and thinly sliced
12 ripe olives, sliced
1 green pepper, seeded and finely chopped
3 green onions, thinly sliced
Garnish: strips of pimiento and hard-cooked egg whites

Remove yolks of eggs and mash with olive oil to make a smooth paste. Stir in garlic, Worcestershire sauce, mustard, Tabasco, and lemon juice.

Add seasonings to sieved tomatoes, along with cucumber, avocado, olives, green pepper, and green onions.

Chill in refrigerator. Garnish with strips of hard-cooked egg whites and pimiento before serving.

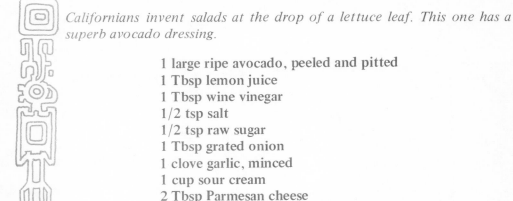

Californians invent salads at the drop of a lettuce leaf. This one has a superb avocado dressing.

1 large ripe avocado, peeled and pitted
1 Tbsp lemon juice
1 Tbsp wine vinegar
1/2 tsp salt
1/2 tsp raw sugar
1 Tbsp grated onion
1 clove garlic, minced
1 cup sour cream
2 Tbsp Parmesan cheese
1/2 head iceberg lettuce
1/2 head romaine
6 green onions, sliced
1 cup fresh, garlic-flavored croutons
2 hard-cooked eggs, chopped

Mash avocado with fork. Mix avocado with lemon juice, vinegar, salt, sugar, onion, garlic, sour cream, and cheese. Cover with plastic wrap and let dressing stand for several hours.

Wash iceberg and romaine lettuce; break into bite-size pieces. Put lettuce in a salad bowl with green onions, and croutons. Toss salad with avocado dressing, and sprinkle with chopped eggs. If you like, grind a little black pepper over top.

Avocado Cake — For Real

*Would you believe avocado cake? It looks and tastes like a spicy choco-
late cake, but it has the delicate smoothness of avocado. (Note that
carob is used in place of chocolate.)*

3/4 cup margarine
2 cups raw sugar
3 eggs, beaten
1 3/4 cups whole wheat pastry flour
1/3 cup carob
3/4 tsp allspice
3/4 tsp cinnamon
3/4 tsp salt
1 1/2 tsp baking soda
1 1/2 cups mashed avocado
3/4 cup buttermilk
1 cup walnuts, chopped
1/4 cup whole wheat pastry flour

Cream margarine and sugar together until mixture is light and fluffy.
Slowly add eggs, beating well.

Sift together flour, carob, allspice, cinnamon, salt, and baking soda.
Add dry ingredients to egg-sugar mixture, and beat well. Stir in avocado
and buttermilk. Mix walnuts with flour and stir into batter.

Pour batter into a greased, 8-inch square pan. Bake in a 350 degree
oven for 50 minutes, or until done.

Mediterranean Eggplant

Olive orchards are as old as civilization. The rich, pungent olive is the soul and sorcery of Mediterranean cooking. Taste for yourself.

1 large eggplant, peeled
3 eggs, beaten
1 cup dried bread crumbs
3/4 cup olive oil
3 cups tomato sauce
1 tsp oregano

1 tsp basil
1 tsp salt
1/2 cup black sliced olives
1/2 tsp black pepper
2/3 cup Parmesan cheese, grated
1/2 lb Mozzarella cheese, thinly sliced

Cut eggplant into 1/4-inch slices. Dip slices first in egg and then in bread crumbs.

Heat olive oil in skillet and saute eggplant on both sides until golden brown.

In a saucepan combine tomato sauce with oregano, basil, salt, olives, and pepper. Simmer 5 minutes.

Place a layer of eggplant in a casserole; sprinkle over a little of the Parmesan cheese, and top with a layer of Mozzarella slices. Spoon over a little of the tomato-olive sauce. Repeat layers of eggplant, Parmesan cheese, Mozzarella, and sauce until eggplant is used up. End final layer with Mozzarella cheese and pour remaining sauce over top.

Bake, uncovered, in a 350 degree oven for 30 minutes, or until sauce is bubbly and cheese is melted.

Classic Greek Salad

An ancient Greek proverb proclaims that a long and pleasant life depends on two fluids, wine and olive oil. This salad has both.

1 head iceberg lettuce, broken into bite-size pieces
1 cucumber, thinly sliced
2 ripe tomatoes, cut into quarters
1 cup Greek Feta cheese, diced
12 black Greek olives, pitted
1 small red onion, thinly sliced
1/2 cup cooked beets, diced and drained
1 Tbsp capers
1 tsp oregano
1/2 cup light olive oil
4 Tbsp wine vinegar
1/2 tsp salt
1/4 tsp fresh ground pepper
1 tsp dry mustard
1 Tbsp fresh minced basil
  or 1 tsp dried basil

In a salad bowl combine lettuce, cucumber, tomatoes, Feta cheese, olives, onion, beets, and capers.

Mix together oregano, olive oil, wine vinegar, salt, pepper, and mustard. Pour over salad and toss well. Sprinkle basil over top.

Missionaries brought the olive to Mexico in the 17th century—just in time to flavor this lively tamale.

1 onion, finely chopped
1 green pepper, seeded, finely chopped
2 Tbsp margarine
3 cups cooked, boned chicken
2 cups tomato sauce
1 1/2 cups fresh corn kernels
1 cup whole pitted black olives
1 clove garlic, minced

1 tsp salt
3 tsp chili powder
1/8 tsp Tabasco Sauce
1 1/2 cups Cheddar cheese, grated
3/4 cup yellow corn meal
1/2 tsp salt
2 cups cold water
2 Tbsp butter

Saute onion and green pepper in margarine until soft. Add chicken, tomato sauce, corn kernels, olives, garlic, salt, chili powder, and Tabasco Sauce. Simmer for 10 minutes. Stir in cheese, and keep stirring until cheese melts.

Pour into a shallow casserole.

Combine corn meal, salt, and cold water in a saucepan. Cook until corn meal thickens. Stir in butter. Spoon corn meal topping over casserole.

Bake in a 350 degree oven for 40 minutes or until topping browns.

Fresh Corn Casserole

When Father Junipero Serra established the first chain of motels in California, olives became a mission fruit. Try the venerable olive in a zesty western casserole.

4 Tbsp margarine
2 cups fresh corn kernels
1/2 cup green bell pepper, seeded and chopped
1/4 cup pimientos, chopped
1/2 cup pitted green olives, sliced
2 Tbsp parsley, minced
4 Tbsp whole wheat pastry flour
1 tsp salt
1/2 tsp pepper
2 cups milk
3 eggs, beaten
1 cup grated Cheddar cheese

Melt margarine and stir in corn kernels, green bell pepper, pimientos, olives, and parsley. Saute for 2 minutes; cover, and simmer for 10 minutes, stirring frequently.

Stir in flour, salt, and pepper. Gradually add milk, and cook until vegetable mixture thickens. Cool slightly; beat in eggs, and cheese.

Pour into a greased casserole. Set casserole in a pan of water and bake in a 350 degree oven for 30 minutes.

CHAPTER II

THE WORLD IN A NUTSHELL

Travel to India for a Cashew Curry, or to France for a Shrimp Amandine. Dine like an ancient Roman on Jupiter's Walnut Chicken, or come into the Casbah for an Algerian chicken with pistachios. It's a wonderfully nutty world, so make the most of it!

Nuts add a wonderful crunch and flavor to almost everything, including vegetables, noodles, and Chinese stir-fries.

Chinese Almond Chicken

In ancient mythology, the almond tree figured as the father of all things, being the first to flower in the spring. Almonds are still sacred to cooks—especially the Chinese.

2 chicken breasts, cooked
3 Tbsp vegetable oil
1/2 tsp salt
1/4 tsp pepper
3 Tbsp soy sauce
1 cup celery, diced
1 cup Chinese peas

1/2 cup green onions, finely sliced
1 cup fresh mushrooms, sliced
1/2 cup water chestnuts
1/2 cup blanched almonds, toasted
1 cup chicken broth, heated
2 Tbsp cornstarch
2 Tbsp water

Skin and bone chicken breasts; cut meat into small strips.

Heat oil in a Chinese wok, or skillet, and saute chicken for 3 minutes, stirring constantly.

Season chicken with salt, pepper, and soy sauce. Add peas, green onions, mushrooms, water chestnuts, and almonds. Stir and cook for 2 minutes. Pour in hot chicken broth.

Cover pan, and simmer over low heat for another 5 minutes.

Mix cornstarch and water into a paste; stir it into chicken-vegetable mixture. Simmer another minute until sauce thickens a little.

Serve with, or over, rice.

Almond Sour Cream Sauce

Careme, the great 18th century chef, proclaimed that almonds sweetened the bitterness of humors. Almonds also have the power to charm vegetables in this velvety almond sauce.

1/2 cup raw almond butter
1/2 cup sour cream
1 Tbsp honey
1/4 tsp salt
1 Tbsp lemon juice

    Combine all ingredients; stir well until sauce is smooth and well blended.

    This sauce is especially delicious spooned over green beans, peas, or summer squash.

    (Almond butter may be purchased at health food stores.)

Shrimp Amandine

In the hands of the French, almonds browned in butter or margarine make a masterful topping called amandine.

1 1/2 cups small-curd cottage cheese
2 Tbsp dry sherry
2 Tbsp Parmesan cheese, grated
1 Tbsp Worcestershire sauce
1 Tbsp lemon juice
1/2 tsp salt
1/4 tsp white pepper
2 lbs cooked shrimp, shelled & deveined
1/2 cup fine bread crumbs
6 Tbsp margarine
1/3 cup blanched, sliced almonds

In a bowl mix together cottage cheese, sherry, Parmesan cheese, Worcestershire sauce, lemon juice, salt, and pepper.

Spoon shrimp equally into 4 individual, oiled casseroles. Spread cottage cheese mixture equally over shrimp. Sprinkle tops of casseroles with bread crumbs.

Melt margarine in a skillet, and saute almonds until lightly browned. Spoon melted margarine and almonds over bread crumbs.

Bake casseroles in a 350 degree oven for 10 to 15 minutes until ingredients are hot and cheese begins to soften.

Far Out Noodles

Out West, the California almond gives crunch to a quiet noodle casserole.

8 oz **medium-width** noodles
2 **Tbsp salt**
2 cups **cottage cheese**
2 cups **sour cream**
1/4 cup **margarine**, melted
1/4 cup **green onions**, finely chopped
1 clove **garlic**, minced
1 tsp **Worcestershire** Sauce
Dash of Tabasco Sauce
1/2 **tsp salt**
1/4 **tsp pepper**
1/3 cup **Parmesan** cheese, grated
1/3 cup **blanched**, chopped almonds, toasted

Cook noodles in boiling salted water for 8 minutes. Drain, and flush noodles quickly in cold water.

In a bowl combine cottage cheese, sour cream, margarine, green onions, garlic, Worcestershire Sauce, Tabasco, salt, and pepper. Stir cheese mixture into noodles, and transfer into a greased casserole.

Spoon Parmesan cheese over top; cover, and bake in a 350 degree oven for 30 minutes. Sprinkle top with almonds, and continue baking another 10 minutes.

Jupiter's Walnut Chicken

Before English walnuts became English, they were called Jupiter's Acorns. The Romans regarded walnuts as food for the Gods. Help yourself to an Olympian chicken.

2 frying chickens, cut in serving-size pieces
1/2 cup cracker crumbs
1/2 cup Parmesan cheese, grated
1/2 cup walnuts, finely chopped
3 Tbsp parsley, minced
2 eggs, beaten
4 Tbsp margarine
1 tsp salt
1/2 tsp pepper
1/4 cup walnuts, finely chopped

Remove skin from chicken pieces; bone breasts.

In a bowl, mix together cracker crumbs, cheese, walnuts, and parsley. Dip chicken first in egg, and then in crumb mixture—making sure the chicken is generously coated.

Melt margarine in skillet, and saute chicken until golden brown.

Arrange chicken in a single layer in a shallow baking pan. Season with salt and pepper.

Cover, and bake in a 350 degree oven for 1 hour, or until tender. Ten minutes before chicken is cooked, sprinkle additional walnuts over the top. Garnish with paprika.

Bewitching Walnut Bread

Some say that witches like to meet under walnut trees—which may explain the bewitching flavor of this walnut-onion bread.

2 1/2 cups whole wheat pastry flour
1 Tbsp raw sugar
1/2 Tbsp salt
2 Packages fresh, active dry yeast
1 cup lukewarm milk
1/4 cup margarine, melted
1/3 cup onions, finely chopped
1/3 cup walnuts, finely chopped

Sift together flour, sugar and salt.

Dissolve yeast in 1/2 cup of lukewarm milk. Stir dissolved yeast into flour mixture, and beat in 1/2 cup of remaining milk with margarine.

Knead dough for 10 minutes until it is smooth.

Cover bowl, and let dough rise in a warm place for 2 hours.

Punch down dough, and add onions and walnuts. Divide dough and put each half into a greased loaf pan. Let rise for 45 minutes.

Bake loaves in a 400 degree oven for 45 minutes, or until cooked and golden brown. Cool loaves on a wire rack.

Spinach Walnut Souffle

Spinach is a dinner—when you add walnuts.

3 cups cooked, chopped spinach, well drained
1/2 cup bread crumbs
3/4 cup walnuts, finely chopped
1/4 cup margarine, melted
1/2 tsp salt
1/4 tsp pepper
3 eggs, well beaten

In a bowl, combine spinach, bread crumbs, walnuts, margarine, salt, and pepper. Beat in eggs.

Pour into a greased souffle dish, and bake in a preheated 375 degree oven for 30 minutes, or until firm.

Since the walnut became a native Californian, it loves burgers. This one is vegetarian, but hearty!

2 Tbsp margarine	1 tsp Worcestershire Sauce
3 Tbsp onion, minced	1/4 tsp thyme
1 cup toasted walnuts, finely chopped	1/4 tsp sage
1/3 cup cooked brown rice	1/2 tsp salt
1/2 cup whole wheat bread crumbs	1/4 tsp ground black pepper
2 Tbsp parsley, minced	1 egg, beaten
2 Tbsp tomato paste	2 tbsp margarine

Melt margarine in a skillet, and saute onions a few minutes.

Stir onions into a bowl with walnuts, cooked brown rice, bread crumbs, parsley, tomato paste, Worcestershire Sauce, thyme, sage, salt, pepper, and egg. Blend well.

Shape mixture into patties using 1/3 of a cup of mixture for each patty. Chill for 30 minutes.

Melt margarine in a skillet, and brown walnut burgers on both sides.

Spoon Cheddar Cheese Sour Cream Sauce on patties before serving. See recipe on page 54

Orange Pecan Sweet Potatoes

Pecan orchards thrive on Southern hospitality from Virginia to Texas. Have a taste of the new south in a sweet potato casserole that's layered with oranges and topped with pecans.

4 cooked, peeled sweet potatoes
2 oranges, peeled
1 Tbsp cornstarch
3 Tbsp margarine
1/3 cup raw sugar
1 tsp molasses
1/2 tsp salt
1 cup fresh orange juice
1 Tbsp orange peel, finely chopped
1/3 cup pecan halves

Slice sweet potatoes crosswise into 1-inch thick slices. Slice oranges into 1/4-inch slices.

Arrange potatoes and orange slices in a greased casserole in alternate layers.

In a bowl, mix together cornstarch and margarine. Add sugar, molasses, salt, orange juice, and orange peel.

Pour into a skillet, and simmer until sauce thickens and is smooth.

Pour sauce over casserole. Sprinkle pecan halves over top.

Bake in a 350 degree oven for 25 minutes.

Happy Hour's Cheese

After a hard day picking profits on the cotton exchange, Southerners welcome the happy hour with this savory cheese hors d'oeuvre.

1 large **Edam or Gouda cheese**
1/2 cup **sour cream**
2 Tbsp **chives, chopped**
1/2 tsp **onion salt**
1/4 tsp **Tabasco Sauce**
1/4 cup **pecans, finely chopped**

   Slice top off Edam or Gouda cheese, cutting rim into saw-tooth pattern. Scoop out cheese leaving a 1/2-inch shell inside.
   Shred cheese and blend with sour cream, chives, onion salt, and Tabasco. Blend until cheese is a creamy consistency. (Spices may be increased according to taste.)
   Spoon cheese mixture back into cheese shell; wrap in foil paper and refrigerate a few hours. Before serving, sprinkle pecans over the top.

Stuffed Artichokes with Pine Nuts

Whatever you call 'em—Indian nuts, pinions, pignolas, or pine nuts—these tasty little nuggets of the pine tree are native to many kitchens. Here they season an Italian artichoke.

4 large artichokes
1 cup cooked brown rice
2 Tbsp parsley, minced
2 green onions, thinly sliced
8 mushrooms, sliced
1/2 cup Parmesan cheese, grated
1/4 cup shelled pine nuts, toasted

1 tsp oregano
1 tsp salt
6 Tbsp olive oil
1 1/2 cup water
1/4 cup lemon juice
1/2 tsp salt

Soak artichokes in cold, salted water for 30 minutes.

Cut off stems and outside bottom row of leaves. Cut off the top third of each artichoke. Force leaves apart and scoop out feathery chokes with a melon-ball scooper, or sharp spoon.

Mix together rice, parsley, onions, mushrooms, cheese, pine nuts, oregano, salt and 2 Tbsp of olive oil. Pack stuffing into center of hollowed-out artichokes, and between the leaves.

Arrange artichokes in pan small enough to hold them snugly upright. Add water, and drizzle artichokes with remaining oil and lemon juice. Season with salt.

Cover and simmer for 30 minutes, or until artichokes are tender. Add more water if needed.

Barley Bowl

Praise Demeter, the Barley Mother, for her nourishing cereal that tastes so good with pine nuts.

1/2 cup celery, finely chopped
1/3 cup green onions, finely chopped
1/4 cup green pepper, finely chopped
5 Tbsp margarine
1 cup barley
1/3 cup parsley, finely chopped
2 cups chicken broth
1/2 cup shelled pine nuts

Saute celery, onions, and green pepper in margarine until vegetables are soft. Add barley, and stir until lightly browned. Season with parsley and spoon into a greased casserole.

Pour in 1 cup of chicken broth; cover, and bake for 30 minutes in a 350 degree oven. Add 1 more cup of broth, sprinkle casserole with pine nuts. Continue baking, uncovered, for 3 minutes, or until barley is cooked. If necessary, add more chicken broth.

Chestnuts are what you make them. Try them as a soup, stuffing, salad, dessert, and most of all, as a vegetable with creamed mushrooms.

1 lb chestnuts
1 lb mushrooms
1/4 cup margarine
2 Tbsp whole wheat pastry flour
1 1/2 cups half-and-half
1/2 tsp salt
1/4 tsp pepper
Garnish: chopped parsley

Use a sharp knife to slash the flat side of the chestnut shell.

Place chestnuts in saucepan, cover with water and boil for 15 or 20 minutes. Drain nuts, remove outer shell and inner brown skin. (Chestnuts are easier to peel when hot.) Quarter nuts and reserve.

Remove tough tip of mushroom stems. Quarter mushrooms.

In a skillet, melt margarine, and saute mushrooms until lightly browned. Mix in flour, and stir well. Gradually add half-and-half, then season with salt & pepper. Add chestnuts, and simmer until sauce bubbles and ingredients are hot.

Garnish with parsley before serving.

Moongate Chicken

In the orient the chestnut is celebrated in a number of dishes. This is one of the best.

1 frying chicken
1 tsp salt
1/4 tsp pepper
4 Tbsp soy sauce
4 Tbsp sherry
3 Tbsp vegetable oil
1 tsp ginger root, minced
8 green onions, thinly sliced
1 cup chicken stock
1 cup cooked, shelled chestnuts

Have butcher cut chicken in small serving pieces; cut the breast into four parts.

In a bowl, combine salt, pepper, soy sauce, and sherry. Marinate chicken pieces in this sauce for 1 or 2 hours; turning chicken so it is well coated with the marinade.

Heat oil in a Chinese wok, or large skillet, and quickly brown chicken. Add ginger root, onions, and chicken stock. Cover pan and simmer over low heat for 30 minutes. Add more stock if necessary. Stir in chestnuts. and continue simmering another 15 minutes, or until chicken is tender.

Spoon out chicken, onions, and chestnuts onto platter; and serve with rice.

Cashew Stuffing

Cashews have a quiet crunchiness that's perfect for quiet little dinners. Use them in rice stuffings for gala birds.

3 Tbsp margarine, melted
1/2 onion, finely chopped
1/3 cup celery, diced
2 cups cooked brown rice
1 cup cashew nuts, coarsely chopped
4 sprigs parsley, chopped
3 Tbsp sherry
1/2 tsp pepper
1/4 tsp ground ginger.
1/4 tsp ground mace
1/4 tsp thyme

Melt margarine in a skillet, and saute onion until soft.

In a bowl combine onion, celery, rice, nuts, and parsley. Season stuffing with sherry, pepper, ginger, mace, and thyme. Toss stuffing well until flavors are blended.

Spoon stuffing lightly into the cavity of fowl, allowing room for expansion. Close opening with skewers before roasting bird.

Vegetable Cashew Curry

The cashew nut is sacred to the curry ritual. It serves as a condiment, and in some curries, as a basic ingredient.

> 1/4 cup margarine
> 1/2 tsp salt
> 1 Tbsp curry powder
> 1 cup chicken broth
> 2 potatoes, peeled and cubed
> 1 cup green beans, cut into 1-inch lengths
> 1 tomato, peeled and chopped
> 1/2 cup green onions, finely sliced
> 1 small head cauliflower, broken into flowerets
> 1/2 cup fresh peas, shelled
> 1/3 cup cashews, halved

Melt margarine in a saucepan and add salt, curry powder, and chicken broth. When broth is simmering, add potatoes, green beans, tomato and onions.

Cover, and simmer 10 minutes.

Add cauliflower; cover, and simmer another 10 minutes.

Stir in peas, and continue to simmer vegetables, uncovered, for 10 minutes more, or until vegetables are cooked and liquid is reduced. Add cashews a few minutes before serving.

If you like a spicier curry, feel free to increase the curry powder.

Sesame Wheat Pilaf

Pistachios garnish an Arabian bulgur wheat pilaf flavored with sesame seeds. You can eat this for a thousand-and-one-nights and never get bored.

1/2 onion, finely chopped
1/4 cup vegetable oil
1 cup bulgur wheat
1/4 cup sesame seeds, toasted
2 cups chicken stock
1 tsp salt
1 Tbsp parsley, finely chopped
1 whole garlic clove
1/3 cup shelled pistachio nuts, finely chopped

Saute onion in vegetable oil until soft. Add bulgur wheat and sesame seeds; stir until wheat is coated with oil. Add stock, salt, parsley, and garlic clove. Cover and simmer until pilaf is cooked. Remove garlic clove.
Sprinkle with pistachio nuts.

Honey Chicken with Pistachio Nuts

The Queen of Sheba was so fond of pistachio nuts she kept a private orchard for her personal use. You don't need a royal orchard, or even a tree, to produce this pistachio chicken.

1 5 lb roasting chicken
1/2 cup margarine
6 Tbsp sage honey
1 Tbsp dry mustard
1/2 tsp cinnamon
1 whole onion, studded with 2 cloves
1 tsp salt
1/3 cup shelled pistachios, finely chopped

Prick breast and legs of chicken with a fork.

Mix together margarine, honey, mustard and cinnamon and slather over chicken.

Season chicken cavity with salt and place onion inside. Truss chicken.

Put chicken in a roasting pan, and roast in a 350 degree oven for 2 hours, or until tender. Baste frequently.

Dust bird with pistachios before serving.

Coconut Shrimp Curry

In India, coconuts are regarded as the fruit of Sri, the Goddess of prosperity. This shrimp curry has a wealth of coconut flavor.

2 coconuts
*1 1/2 cups coconut "milk"
1/4 cup onion, finely chopped
6 Tbsp margarine
6 Tbsp whole wheat pastry flour
2 Tbsp curry powder

2 cups half-and-half
1 tsp ground ginger
2 Tbsp lemon juice
2 tsp salt
2 lbs fresh, cooked shrimp, shelled
   and deveined

Pierce "eyes" of coconuts and drain liquid into a saucepan. Add sufficient dairy milk to make 1 1/2 cups of coconut "milk."

Crack coconut shell, remove meat and grate it into coconut "milk." Heat until hot; remove pan from stove and let liquid stand 30 minutes. Strain the "milk," and reserve the grated coconut to serve later with the curry.

Saute onion in margarine until soft; stir in flour, and curry powder. Slowly add coconut "milk" and half-and-half; then simmer over low heat until sauce thickens. Season with ginger, lemon juice, and salt. Stir in cooked shrimp. Simmer for 10 minutes stirring frequently.

Serve over rice with side condiments of grated coconut, chopped cashews, chopped hard-cooked eggs, and chopped green onions.

*Coconut milk may be purchased at food stores, if you can't make your own.

Classified Chicken Curry

Everyone has their secret recipe for chicken curry. Here's ours. The secret is a touch of tomato paste and chopped orange peel—in addition to the sacred coconut. (Don't tell anyone.)

1 onion, finely chopped
1/4 cup margarine
6 Tbsp whole wheat pastry flour
2 Tbsp curry powder
3 cups chicken broth
2 Tbsp tomato paste
1 apple, peeled, cored and grated
2 Tbsp orange rind, chopped

1 clove garlic, chopped
*1/2 cup coconut "milk"
1/2 cup half-and-half
3 cups cooked, boned chicken, cut
  into bite-size pieces
1/2 cup blanched, slivered
  almonds, toasted

Saute onion in margarine until soft. Stir in flour and curry powder and blend well. Slowly add chicken broth, and simmer until sauce thickens. Add tomato paste, apple, chopped orange rind, and garlic.

Simmer a few minutes, then stir in coconut "milk" and half-and-half. Add chicken; and simmer another 10 minutes, stirring frequently.

Serve over rice and sprinkle with almonds.

*Use the basic recipe for coconut "milk" on page xx. However, for 1/2 cup of "milk" only 1 coconut is required.

Granola with Coconut

Here's another way to get your daily minimum requirement of coconut prosperity.

1 1/2 lbs rolled oats
1 cup shredded coconut
1 cup mixed chopped nuts
  (almonds, pecans, and walnuts)
1/4 cup unsliced, hulled
  sunflower seeds
1 cup wheat germ
1 tsp salt
3/4 cup safflower oil

1/3 cup water
1 1/2 Tbsp vanilla
3/4 cup honey
1 cup golden raisins
1/2 cup pitted dates, coarsely
  chopped
1/2 cup dried apricots, coarsely
  chopped

In a bowl combine rolled oats, shredded coconut, mixed nuts, sun-flower seeds, wheat germ, and salt.

Beat together oil, water, vanilla, and honey until well blended. Pour liquid into cereal mixture and stir until mixture is thoroughly coated.

Spread granola 1/2 inch thick on an oiled cookie sheet. Bake in a slow oven (250 degrees) for about 1 1/2 hours. Turn the granola completely after the first half hour, and again every 15 minutes so the cereal is completely toasted to a golden brown.

Remove from oven and turn the granola over again. Cool. Add raisins, dates and apricots. Keep granola in a tightly closed container in a cool, dry place.

CHAPTER III

SPICE TREE COOKERY

When the world was flat, the cooking was flatter. No wonder Columbus left home in search of spices.

The nicest spices grow on trees, and their names are cinnamon, cloves, nutmeg, and allspice. These lively seasonings add sparkle to a variety of foods other than the usual desserts. Wait until you try a shake of nutmeg, or cinnamon, on vegetables—or a little allspice with fish. Outstanding!

The spice orchard also produces the savory bay leaf, chocolate bean, and carob bean, for which we include a selection of recipes.

85

Clove Cake

According to legend in the Spice Islands, when the clove trees are in bud, no one may wear a hat in the clove orchard or make a loud noise, least the trees be alarmed and drop their buds. The pampered clove makes a memorable cake.

2 3/4 cups whole wheat pastry flour
1 Tbsp powdered cloves
1 Tbsp cinnamon
1 tsp baking powder
1 tsp baking soda
1/2 tsp salt

1 cup golden raisins
1/4 cup whole wheat pastry flour
1 cup margarine, softened
2 1/4 cups raw sugar
5 eggs, beaten
1 cup buttermilk

Sift flour with cloves, cinnamon, baking powder, soda, and salt.
Toss raisins with 1/4 cup flour.
Cream margarine and sugar together. Beat in eggs.
Slowly add buttermilk and dry ingredients, alternately, to sugar-egg mixture, and beat batter until smooth. Stir in raisins.
Pour batter into 10-inch greased tube pan.
Bake in a preheated 350 degree oven for 1 hour, or until done. Cool cake in pan before removing to a wire rack and cooling completely.
If you like a frosting, use the Lemon Honey frosting on page 18

Hot Mulled Wine

Cloves spice a hot mulled wine for skiers and fireside-skiers.

1 qt burgundy or claret
Peel of 1 orange
Peel of 1 lemon
2 inches of cinnamon stick
1 whole nutmeg, crushed
6 whole cloves
1 Tbsp raw sugar

Mix all ingredients in a saucepan, and simmer gently for 5 to 10 minutes. Strain and serve hot in mugs.

Cinnamon Chicken

The warm, bitter sweet cinnamon from Malaysia is more than a dessert spice. Taste what it does for chicken!

2 frying chickens, cut in serving pieces
1 cup whole wheat pastry flour
4 Tbsp margarine
1 tsp salt
1 onion, finely chopped
2-inch cinnamon stick
1/4 tsp mace
1/4 tsp pepper
4 cups chicken stock
1/2 cup white rice
Garnish: minced parsley

Shake chicken pieces in a bag with flour until well coated.

Melt margarine in skillet and lightly brown chicken. Season with salt. Transfer chicken to a saucepan.

Saute onion in skillet until soft.

Spoon onions over chicken and tuck the cinnamon stick among chicken pieces. Season with mace and pepper, then pour in chicken stock.

Cover, and simmer 30 minutes. Add rice; cover, and continue simmering until rice is cooked and chicken is tender.

Garnish with parsley before serving.

Summer Blessing

When you cook fruit, think cinnamon. A stick of cinnamon is the magic ingredient in this medley of summer fruits.

2 cups raw sugar
6 cups water
3 inch cinnamon stick
6 cloves
1/2 pineapple, peeled and cubed
1/2 lb cherries, pitted
2 pears, peeled and sliced
1/2 lb blackberries
1/2 lb peaches, pitted, peeled and quartered
1/2 lb apricots, pitted, peeled and halved
juice of 2 lemons
Garnish: cinnamon

In a saucepan combine sugar, water, cinnamon stick, and cloves. Simmer until hot and add pineapple, cherries, pears, blackberries, peaches, and apricots.

Cover saucepan, and continue simmering fruit over low temperature for 15 minutes, or until fruit is tender.

Discard cloves and cinnamon stick. Stir in lemon juice. Cool. Spoon out fruit into bowls with a little of the syrup and a garnish of cinnamon.

Spicy Acorn Squash

Cinnamon also has a talent for bringing out the unsuspected charms of ordinary vegetables. Never has acorn squash tasted so good.

2 acorn squashes
1 cup water
1/4 cup margarine, melted
1 tsp cinnamon
1/4 tsp nutmeg
1/4 tsp ginger
1/2 tsp salt
1/3 cup honey

Wash squash, and cut in half lengthwise. Remove seeds and stringy fibers.

Place squash halves in shallow baking pan, cut-side down. Pour in 1 cup of water.

Cover pan, and bake 30 minutes in a 350 degree oven.

Pour off excess liquid from pan; turn squash halves cut-side up.

Combine margarine, cinnamon, nutmeg, ginger, salt, and honey; then beat well. Pour honey mixture into squash cavities.

Bake 15 minutes in a 350 degree oven, basting frequently with sauce.

Cinnamon Almond Cookies

How can you miss with a cooky that's spiced with cinnamon, and crunchy with almonds?

1 cup raw sugar
1 Tbsp molasses
1 cup whole wheat pastry flour, sifted
2/3 cup blanched almonds, chopped
1/4 cup margarine, softened
2 tsp cinnamon
1/4 tsp salt
1/4 cup water

In a bowl, blend sugar and molasses. Stir in flour, almonds, margarine, cinnamon, and salt. Add sufficient water to make a stiff dough.

Spoon out batter by the teaspoonful onto a greased cookie sheet, leaving enough room for cookies to spread.

Bake in a 300 degree oven for 15 to 20 minutes, or until cookies are golden brown. Cool on rack.

Squash Cheese Casserole

The whisper of nutmeg in this unusual blend of squash and cheeses is an inspired touch. Try it with freshly ground nutmeg!

2 lb crookneck squash, finely chopped
1 Tbsp salt
1 1/2 cups Cheddar cheese, grated
1 cup cottage cheese
5 eggs, beaten
1 cup bread crumbs
3 Tbsp parsley, chopped
1/2 tsp nutmeg, freshly ground
1/2 tsp pepper
4 Tbsp margarine, melted

Spoon squash into a bowl. Season with salt and leave 15 minutes. Press out all liquid.

Mix in Cheddar cheese, cottage cheese, eggs, bread crumbs. Season with parsley, nutmeg, and pepper.

Pour into a casserole, spoon melted margarine over the top.

Bake in a 350 degree oven for 1 hour, or until firm.

Nutmeg Love Cake

Gypsies vow your wedding knot will never slip if you make this magic potion. Cut a nutmeg into three parts; bury one, throw the second in the fire, and boil the third and drink the brew. (An easier way to save your marriage is to bake him a nutmeg cake.)

2 cups raw sugar
1 Tbsp molasses
1/2 cup margarine
2 cups whole wheat pastry flour, sifted
1/2 tsp salt
1 tsp nutmeg
1 tsp baking soda
1 cup sour cream
1 egg, beaten
1/2 cup pecans, chopped

Stir sugar and molasses together. Cream in margarine and add flour, salt, and nutmeg. Stir with a pastry blender until mixture is crumbly.

Spoon half the crumbly mixture into a greased baking pan.

Stir baking soda into sour cream—together with remaining crumbly mixture. Beat in egg.

Spoon over mixture in the baking pan. Sprinkle with nuts and bake in a 350 degree oven for 45 minutes, or until done.

Jamaica Bananas with Allspice

The allspice tree is alive and living in Jamaica. Allspice is nature's blend of cinnamon, cloves, and nutmeg—and it loves Jamaican baked bananas!

4 large bananas
2 Tbsp lemon juice
6 Tbsp margarine
2 Tbsp dark rum
1/4 cup raw sugar
1 tsp molasses
1 Tbsp Allspice
1/2 cup cashew nuts, finely chopped and browned

Peel bananas and cut them lengthwise into halves. Brush with lemon juice.

Place bananas in a greased, shallow baking pan.

Heat margarine and rum in a skillet, and pour over bananas.

Stir sugar and molasses together and spoon over bananas.

Dust bananas with allspice, and top with cashews.

Bake for 15 minutes in a 350 degree oven.

Jamaican Poached Fish

Mr. Fish, he is so nice with a twist of lemon and a shake of allspice.

1 qt water	4 whole allspice, cracked
1 cup white wine	1 bay leaf
1 Tbsp salt	1/2 onion, sliced
1/2 tsp sugar	2 lbs halibut, 1 inch thick
4 whole black peppercorns	

Combine first seven ingredients in a large skillet, and simmer for 3 minutes.

Place fish steaks gently in broth, one at a time, letting the broth return to simmer. Simmer fish gently until it is cooked and flakes easily when tested with a toothpick. (Do not overcook, 5 minutes is usually sufficient cooking time.)

Remove fish steaks from broth and serve hot, or chilled, with the following seasoned mayonnaise.

ALLSPICE MAYONNAISE

Combine 1 cup mayonnaise with 2 Tbsp chopped parsley, 2 Tbsp lemon juice, and 1 tsp powdered allspice.

Daphne's Marinated Mushrooms

The laurel or bay tree is a living legend. It embodies the spirit of a woodland nymph called Daphne. While fleeing the ardent advances of Apollo, the Gods transformed her into a tree. Thank Daphne for these savory mushrooms flavored with bay leaves.

3 cups chicken stock	1/2 tsp thyme
1 cup dry white wine	1 tsp salt
1 cup olive oil	5 peppercorns
1/2 cup fresh lemon juice	1 lb small firm mushrooms
2 bay leaves	Garnish: chopped parsley and
6 sprigs parsley	lemon slices
2 garlic cloves, minced	

In a saucepan combine stock, wine, oil, lemon juice, bay leaves, parsley, garlic, thyme, salt, and peppercorns. Simmer, covered, for 20 minutes.

Remove tough tips from mushrooms stems, and slice mushrooms lengthwise. Add mushrooms to saucepan; bring to a boil, lower heat, and simmer 5 minutes.

Transfer contents of saucepan into a dish, and let cool to room temperature. Marinate mushrooms for at least 4 hours.

Remove mushrooms with a slotted spoon, and put into a serving dish.

Strain marinade and pour over mushrooms.

Garnish with parsley and lemon slices.

Vegetable Banquet

Laurel leaves crown victories—in the kitchen as well as the field. This vegetable dish is a triumph of seasonings.

1 yellow onion, peeled and thinly sliced
2 potatoes, peeled and thinly sliced
2 green peppers, seeded and sliced
1/2 lb string beans, cut in 2-inch lengths
2 small zucchini, sliced
1 small eggplant, peeled and cubed
2 large tomatoes, cut in wedges
1/3 cup olive oil

1 cup vegetable stock
1/4 cup parsley, chopped
1 clove garlic, minced
1/4 tsp cinnamon
1/4 tsp powdered cloves
2 bay leaves
2 tsp salt
1/2 lb sliced mozzarella
      cheese

In a shallow baking dish, layer onion, potatoes, green peppers, string beans, zucchini, eggplant, and tomatoes.

Mix olive oil and vegetable stock and pour over vegetables. Season with parsley, garlic, cinnamon, and cloves. Tuck in bay leaves.

Cover tightly and bake 45 minutes, or until vegetables are tender. Season with salt.

Cover vegetable dish with thin slices of cheese, and place dish under the broiler until cheese melts.

Mexican Hot Chocolate

The bean of the cacao, or chocolate tree, which also grows in the spice orchard, yields the national drink of Mexico. According to legend, Montezuma drank 50 pitchers a day of this Mexican chocolat. What a way to go!

6 oz unsweetened baking chocolate,
   or 6 squares Mexican chocolate
6 cups milk
1 tsp cinnamon
6 Tbsp raw sugar
1 egg
1 tsp vanilla

Grate chocolate, and dissolve in 1/2 cup scalded milk. Stir in cinnamon and sugar. (If Mexican chocolate is used, omit cinnamon since it has cinnamon in it.) Stir in rest of the milk, and simmer 2 minutes. Remove from stove.

Beat egg and vanilla together; continue beating while slowly pouring in the chocolate milk. Heat, but do not boil.

Before serving, beat chocolate with an egg beater to whip up a froth on top.

Carob Fondue

While carob tastes like chocolate, carob is its own bean with its own delicate flavor. This dessert fondue has a wee touch of orange you'll love.

8 oz carob bar
1/3 cup light cream
1/4 cup orange honey
2 Tbsp margarine
1/4 tsp salt
1 tsp orange peel, grated
3 Tbsp fresh orange juice

In a fondue pot, melt carob over a low flame, stirring until smooth. Stir in cream, honey, margarine, salt, orange peel, add orange juice. Simmer until mixture is smooth and bubbly; keep fondue warm over a low flame.

Serve with a platter of fresh fruit dips: apples, pineapple, banana and strawberries. Also serve whole nuts: almonds, walnuts, chestnuts.

100

CHAPTER IV

THE FIELD KITCHEN

   Step over the stone wall into the field kitchen. It's loaded with good things to pick, eat, or cook—everything from sunny melons to bright berries.

   While berries aren't as wild as they were in Grandma's day, they still inspire wild desserts like old-fashioned, down home Strawberry Short-cake or Blackberry Cobbler.

   This chapter also includes recipes for the giant sunflower and friendly peanut.

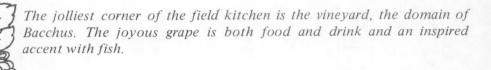

The jolliest corner of the field kitchen is the vineyard, the domain of Bacchus. The joyous grape is both food and drink and an inspired accent with fish.

1/4 cup margarine
2 lb filet of sole
1/2 tsp salt
2 Tbsp lemon juice
1/2 tsp tarragon
1 cup dry white wine
3/4 cup seedless white grapes
1/4 tsp lemon peel, finely chopped
Garnish: paprika and minced parsley

Melt margarine in skillet, and briefly saute fish filets on both sides until lightly browned. Season with salt, lemon juice, and tarragon. Pour in white wine; and gently simmer fish 5 minutes, or less, until it is cooked and easily flakes with a fork.

Remove fish to a platter and keep warm.

Cut grapes in half, or if you're ambitious, peel grapes and leave them whole. Add grapes to skillet with lemon peel, and briefly heat for a few minutes.

Spoon wine sauce and grapes over fish. Garnish with paprika and parsley.

Stuffed Grape Leaves

Stuff a grape leaf with seasoned rice, and you have a succulent morsel. The Greeks have a name for it: Dolmas.

1 large jar grape leaves
2 small onions, finely chopped
1/3 cup olive oil
1 cup brown rice
1 tsp salt
2 1/2 cups water
1/4 cup parsley, finely chopped
1/4 cup currants

1/4 cup walnuts, finely chopped
1/4 cup tomato sauce
1/4 cup water
1/2 tsp allspice
1/4 tsp cinnamon
1/4 tsp pepper
1/2 cup white wine

Rinse grape leaves in cold water.

Saute onions in olive oil until soft, and stir in rice. Add salt and water; simmer rice for 45 minutes, or until cooked. Add parsley, currants, walnuts, tomato sauce, water, allspice, cinnamon, pepper; simmer another 5 minutes. Cool.

Spoon 1 tsp of filling in the center of each grape leaf, and fold into neat packets tucking in ends.

Place dolmas close together in a casserole, weighing them down with an oven-proof plate on top. Pour in white wine, and sufficient water just to cover plate.

Cover and bake in a 300 degree oven for 45 minutes. Cool dolmas in casserole before removing.

Raisin Sesame Cookies

Here's the grape as a raisin in a super healthy cooky that's both nutritious and delicious.

> 1 1/4 cups whole wheat pastry flour, sifted
> 1/2 tsp baking soda
> 1/2 tsp salt
> 1 tsp cinnamon
> 3/4 cup raisins
> 1/2 cup vegetable oil
> 1 cup raw sugar
> 1 large egg, beaten
> 1 1/4 cups rolled oats
> 1 cup sesame seeds
> 1/4 cup milk

Sift flour again with baking soda, salt, and cinnamon. Stir in raisins.

Beat together oil, sugar, and egg. Add rolled oats, sesame seeds, and milk.

Gradually beat in flour mixture, and stir dough until thoroughly blended.

Drop dough by the heaping teaspoonfuls onto a greased cooky sheet, allowing room for the cookies to spread.

Bake in a 375 degree oven for 10 to 15 minutes. Cool cookies before serving.

Currants are tiny raisins with a larger-than-life-size flavor.

4 large tomatoes
1 tsp salt
4 green onions, finely sliced
2 Tbsp olive oil
1 cup cooked brown rice
1/4 tsp basil
1/2 tsp oregano
1 Tbsp parsley, finely chopped
4 Tbsp currants
3 Tbsp shelled pine nuts
1/3 cup Parmesan cheese, grated
1 cup water

Cut tops from tomatoes, and scoop out pulp, leaving 1/4-inch shell. Chop pulp and reserve. Sprinkle shells with salt, and invert to drain.

Saute onions in olive oil a few minutes. Stir onions and oil into cooked rice, and season with basil, oregano, parsley, currants, and pine nuts.

Combine tomato pulp with rice, and spoon stuffing into tomato shells. Sprinkle top with cheese, and replace tomato tops. Set tomatoes in a baking dish, and add water.

Bake tomatoes for 20 to 30 minutes in a 350 degree oven. Check to see that pan liquid doesn't evaporate. Serve hot or cold.

Grape & Orange Marmalade

The versatile grape also has a talent as a marmalade.

1 large navel orange
3/4 cup water
2 cups seedless white grapes
1 1/2 cups raw sugar
1 Tbsp lemon juice

Cut orange and rind into very thin pieces.

Soak orange several hours in water. Add grapes, and soak 30 minutes longer.

Transfer fruit and water to a saucepan; simmer for 5 minutes. Add sugar and lemon juice; simmer another 5 minutes.

Grape Ambrosia

Bacchus named his three sons Grape, Wine-Drinker, and Blooming.
This ambrosial dessert is dedicated to Grape.

1 1/2 lb seedless white grapes
1 cup sour cream
1/3 cup orange honey
3 tsp lemon juice

Wash grapes and remove stems.
In a bowl combine sour cream, honey, and lemon juice.
Just before serving, toss grapes in sour cream sauce, and spoon into
dessert cups.

Pumpkin Soup

The good earth yields another fruit of the vine that grew in wild abundance in the new world, the field pumpkin. This early American fruit/vegetable makes a super soup.

2 Tbsp margarine
1/2 green pepper, seeded and chopped
1 large tomato, chopped
2 green onions, including tops, finely chopped
1 Tbsp parsley, finely chopped
1/4 tsp thyme
1 bay leaf
2 cups cooked pumpkin puree
3 cups chicken stock
1 Tbsp whole wheat pastry flour
1/2 cup milk
1/2 tsp nutmeg
1/2 tsp sugar
1/2 tsp salt, or more, to taste

Melt margarine and simmer green pepper, tomato, and onions, parsley, thyme, and bay leaf for 5 minutes. Stir in pumpkin puree and chicken stock; continue simmering for 30 minutes. Strain mixture through a sieve, and return liquid to pan.

Blend flour and milk together; stir into soup. Season with nutmeg, sugar, and salt. Simmer soup another 5 minutes, then serve.

The Great Pumpkin Loaf

Try the great pumpkin in a rich, spicy bread. It's more of a treat than a trick to make.

6 Tbsp margarine
1 cup raw sugar
1 Tbsp molasses
2 eggs, beaten
1 cup cooked pumpkin puree
2 cups whole wheat pastry flour, sifted
2 tsp baking powder
2 tsp cocoa

1 tsp cinnamon
1/4 tsp ginger
1/4 tsp cloves
1/4 tsp salt
1/4 tsp baking soda
1/4 cup milk
3/4 cup walnuts, chopped

Cream margarine and sugar together. Stir in molasses, eggs, and pumpkin puree.

Sift flour again with baking powder, cocoa, cinnamon, ginger, cloves, salt, and baking soda. Gradually stir flour mixture and milk, alternately, into pumpkin mixture. Stir in walnuts.

Pour into a greased loaf pan. Bake in a 350 degree oven for 60 minutes, or until done. Cool loaf before removing from pan.

Persian Melon with Raspberries

Like its country cousin, the pumpkin, the Persian melon lives on the ground. Nevertheless, this delicate pink melon tastes more celestial than terrestrial.

1 Persian melon
2 cups fresh raspberries
1 cup sweet sauterne, or other sweet white wine

Cut a slice from the top of a Persian melon and scoop out pulp and seeds. Reserve slice. Trim off the bottom of the melon to make a base.

Wash berries well and pour over sweet white wine. Spoon berries and wine into melon and replace top. Chill for 3 hours.

For each serving, scoop out a piece of melon with a little of the berries. For an extra-special treat, spoon the melon and berries over vanilla ice cream.

Spicy Cantaloupe Preserve

All good things should be preserved.

1 large ripe cantaloupe
1 cup raw sugar
1/2 cup water
1/4 cup cider vinegar
3-inch stick of cinnamon
4 whole cloves

Cut meat from cantaloupe, and dice into 1-inch cubes.

Put melon meat into a saucepan with sugar, water, vinegar, cinnamon, and cloves. Bring to a boil, and simmer until melon is tender.

Remove melon with slotted spoon, and put into hot, sterilized mason jars. Simmer syrup five minutes longer, and pour over melon. Seal jars.

Hawaiian Pineapple Chicken

The Hawaiian field kitchen is waist-deep in pineapples. This lush fruit stirs fresh flavor into a Hawaiian-Chinese stir fry.

3 Tbsp vegetable oil
2 cups cooked, boned chicken, cut into small chunks
1/2 cup green onions, finely sliced
1/2 cup celery, diced
1/2 cup Macadamia nuts, chopped
2 Tbsp soy sauce
1/2 tsp raw sugar
1/2 cup chicken stock
1 cup fresh pineapple, cut in chunks

Heat oil in Chinese wok, or skillet, and saute chicken, green onions, and celery for 3 minutes. Stir in nuts, soy sauce, sugar, and chicken stock. Cover, and simmer for 5 minutes.

Add pineapple, and simmer another 3 minutes.

If Macadamia nuts are not available, use chopped Brazil nuts.

Kona Pineapple Seafood Salad

Pineapple is cool in a fresh seafood salad; and we mean fresh, *not fresh-canned, fresh-frozen, or fresh-dehydrated.*

· 2 cups fresh pineapple chunks
1 large apple, peeled, cored and diced
3/4 cup cooked crab or lobster, boned
3/4 cup cooked shrimp, shelled and deveined
1/2 cup mayonnaise
1/2 cup sour cream
2 Tbsp lemon juice
1/2 tsp salt
1/2 tsp tarragon
2 Tbsp parsley, chopped
1 Tbsp chives, chopped
Garnish: avocado slices

In a salad bowl, combine pineapple with apple, crab or lobster, and shrimp.

Mix together mayonnaise, sour cream, lemon juice, salt, tarragon, parsley, and chives. Pour dressing over salad, and toss well.

Garnish with avocado slices.

Crunchy Zucchini

*The field peanut is a pea who aspires to be a nut. So use it like a nut—
to add crunch and flavor in vegetable casseroles.*

6 zucchini
3 slices whole wheat bread
1/2 cup milk
1 egg, beaten
1/2 tsp salt
1/4 tsp pepper
1/2 cup peanuts, finely chopped
1/2 cup Cheddar cheese, grated

Steam zucchini until tender-crisp. Chop into small pieces.

Soak bread in milk, and mash bread into a pulp. Mix bread with zucchini. Stir egg into zucchini; season with salt & pepper. Stir in peanuts.

Spoon into a casserole, and sprinkle top with Cheddar cheese.

Bake in a 350 degree oven until cheese melts and ingredients are hot (about 15 minutes).

Peanut Butter Bread

This bread may put peanut butter sandwiches out of business.

2 cups whole wheat pastry flour
3 tsp baking powder
1/2 tsp salt
1/4 cup margarine, softened
1 cup chunky peanut butter, room temperature
3/4 cup raw sugar
1 large egg, beaten
1 tsp vanilla
1 cup milk

Sift together flour, baking powder, and salt.

In a bowl, beat together margarine and peanut butter. Beat in sugar, egg, and vanilla. Add flour mixture, and stir until you have fine crumbs. Stir in milk, and beat batter well.

Pour into a greased loaf pan.

Bake in a 350 degree oven for 55 to 60 minutes, or until loaf is golden brown.

Cool loaf 10 minutes before removing from pan. Cool completely on wire rack before slicing.

Sunflower Cookies

Another treasure from the fields is the giant sunflower that once bloomed in wild profusion. Sunflower seeds grow a very tasty cooky.

1/2 cup margarine
1 cup raw sugar
1 egg, beaten
1/2 tsp vanilla
1 cup whole wheat pastry flour
1/2 tsp salt
1/2 tsp baking soda
1 1/2 cups quick-cooking rolled oats
1/2 cup shelled, salted, sunflower seeds

Cream together margarine and sugar. Beat in egg and vanilla. Stir in unsifted flour, salt, soda, and oats. Mix thoroughly. Blend in sunflower seeds.

Form dough into roll about 1 1/2 inches in diameter. Chill.

Slice dough into 1/4-inch slices and put on an ungreased cooky sheet.

Bake in a 350 degree oven for 10 minutes, or until cookies are done. Cool on wire rack.

Sunflower Bread

Sunflower bread is just what it should be: earthy, coarse-textured, and naturally nourishing.

1 package of fresh, active
   dry yeast
1 cup warm water
1/8 cup vegetable oil
1/8 cup honey
1 tsp salt

2 cups whole wheat pastry flour
1 cup rye flour
1/2 cup shelled sunflower seeds
3 Tbsp vegetable oil
1 tsp cornstarch
1/4 cup water

Dissolve yeast in 1/4 cup warm water. Stir in remaining water, oil, honey, salt, and 1 cup of the whole wheat flour. Beat well; gradually stirring in rye flour. Beat again, and add sunflower seeds. Add enough of the remaining cup of whole wheat flour to form a stiff dough.

Knead dough on floured board until firm and elastic. Place dough in an oiled mixing bowl, turning once to coat dough with oil. Cover, and let rise until it has doubled in size, about 1 hour.

Knead dough again for a few minutes. Shape into a round ball and place on a greased baking sheet. With a sharp knife, cut a few slits on top 1/4-inch deep, and brush loaf with vegetable oil. Let rise until it has doubled in size, about 30 minutes. Brush bread again with oil.

Bake bread in a 375 degree oven for 30 minutes, or until browned and done.

To give the bread a nice glaze, simmer cornstarch and water in a saucepan for 3 minutes, then brush liquid over the loaf the last 15 minutes of baking.

Wild! Blackberry Cobbler

In the 19th century, berry picking was a family outing. The day's yield from the fields simmered into fragrant jams or desserts. Blackberries often ended in a glorious cobbler.

4 cups fresh, washed blackberries	2 Tbsp raw sugar
1 cup raw sugar	1/2 tsp salt
3 Tbsp whole wheat pastry flour	2 tsp baking powder
1/2 tsp cinnamon	1/2 tsp cream of tartar
3 Tbsp margarine	1/2 cup margarine
2 cups whole wheat pastry flour, sifted	1/2 cup milk

Mix blackberries with sugar, and spoon into a greased shallow, rectangular baking dish. Sprinkle fruit with flour; season with cinnamon and dot with margarine.

Sift together flour, sugar, salt, baking powder, and cream of tartar. Cut in margarine with a pastry blender until mixture is the consistency of coarse bread crumbs. Stir in milk, and knead into a ball.

Roll out dough on a floured board 1/4 inch thick in a size large enough to cover blackberries. Place dough over berries and trim edges inside the rim of the pan. Slash a vent in top of crust.

Bake in a 375 degree oven for 30 to 40 minutes until crust is golden brown. Serve with warm cream.

Old Fashioned Strawberry Shortcake

Here's how strawberry shortcake tasted when the biscuits were baked in a cast iron stove, and berries came from the strawberry patch.

4 cups fresh strawberries, hulled and washed
1 cup raw sugar
2 cups whole wheat pastry flour
2 tsp baking powder
1 tsp salt

5 Tbsp margarine
1/2 cup milk
4 Tbsp margarine
Whipped cream

    Slice 2 cups of strawberries into a bowl and mix with 1/2 cup sugar. Put remaining 2 cups of whole berries into a separate bowl with remaining 1/2 cup sugar.

    Sift together flour, baking powder, and salt. With a pastry blender cut margarine into flour until it is coarse and grainy. Stir in milk and knead dough into a ball.

    Roll out dough 1/2 inch thick on floured board. Cut into six 3-inch rounds (you'll have enough biscuits for a couple of second helpings), and place biscuits on baking sheet.

    Bake 15 minutes in a 375 degree oven.

    Split warm biscuits and spread with margarine. Spoon whole berries on bottom half of biscuits and cover with a dollop of whipped cream. Cover with biscuit top. Spoon sliced berries and juice over top of each biscuit, and garnish with another generous dollop of whipped cream.

Blueberry Lemon Cookies

Take note that July is the month when fresh blueberry cookies come in season.

1/2 cup margarine
1 cup raw sugar
1 Tbsp lemon rind, grated
1 egg, beaten
2 cups whole wheat pastry flour
2 tsp baking powder
1/2 tsp salt
1/4 cup milk
1 cup fresh blueberries, washed

Cream margarine and sugar together until smooth. Add lemon rind and egg, and beat well.

Stir together flour, baking powder, and salt. Alternately add flour mixture and milk to margarine-sugar mixture. Stir until smooth.

Fold in blueberries.

Drop batter by the tablespoonful onto a greased cookie sheet.

Bake in a 375 degree oven for 15 minutes, or until cookies are done.

Raspberry Bread

Bake a bread as fragrant and delectable as a raspberry.

2 cups fresh raspberries
2 Tbsp lemon juice
3/4 cup raw sugar
1/2 cup margarine
1 egg, beaten
1/2 cup milk
3 cups whole wheat pastry flour
1/2 tsp salt
2 tsp baking powder
1/2 tsp baking soda

Mash raspberries with a fork, and add lemon juice.

In a bowl, cream sugar and margarine together. Stir in egg and milk.

Sift together flour, salt, baking powder, and baking soda. Stir into sugar-egg mixture, and beat well. Fold in raspberries.

Pour into greased loaf pan; bake in a 350 degree oven for 50 minutes, or until done.

These delicate little pancakes, made of creamy ricotta cheese, share a breakfast plate with fresh raspberries.

1 cup ricotta cheese
3 eggs, beaten
2 Tbsp vegetable oil
1/4 cup whole wheat pastry flour
2 tsp raw sugar
margarine
2 cups fresh raspberries

In a blender combine cheese, eggs, oil, flour, sugar, and salt. Blend until batter is smooth.

Pour batter into 3-inch rounds on a medium-hot, lightly-greased griddle.

When bubbles appear on surface of pancakes, turn and brown lightly on the other side.

Top pancakes with a generous dollop of margarine. Serve with a garnish of fresh raspberries on each plate.

Cranberry Almond Sauce

The pilgrim cranberry is far from puritan. It makes a sinfully delicious sauce, or glaze, for roast ham, chicken, or turkey.

2 cups raw sugar
1 cup water
1 lb raw cranberries
1/2 cup apricot jam
1/4 cup lemon juice
1/3 cup orange juice
1/2 tsp powdered cloves
1/2 tsp cinnamon
1/3 cup blanched, slivered almonds, browned

Combine sugar and water in a saucepan. Bring to a boil, and simmer 5 minutes. Add cranberries, and simmer until skins pop open, 3 to 5 minutes. Remove from stove.

Add apricot jam, lemon juice, orange juice, cloves, and cinnamon. Cool sauce and stir in almonds. Makes 1 qt.

We close with a fruit bread that could run for office. It combines traditional New England cranberries with a liberal helping of California oranges and walnuts, plus a grass roots flavor of wheat germ from the heartlands.

3/4 cup orange honey
3 Tbsp margarine
1 egg, beaten
3 Tbsp orange peel grated
3 cups whole wheat pastry flour
2 tsp baking powder
1 tsp baking soda
1 tsp salt

1 tsp allspice
1 cup raw sugar
2 cups water
1 lb fresh cranberries
1/2 cup orange juice
1/2 cup wheat germ
1 cup walnuts, coarsely chopped

Beat together honey and margarine. Stir in egg and orange peel. Sift together flour, baking powder, soda, salt, and allspice.

Combine sugar and water in a saucepan, and simmer 5 minutes. Put in cranberries, and cook 3 to 5 minutes until skins pop. Drain cranberries, and add orange juice to cranberry syrup. Slowly stir in syrup and flour mixture, alternately, into honey-margarine mixture, and beat well. Stir in wheat germ, cranberries, and walnuts.

Pour into a large greased loaf pan. Bake for 60 minutes in a 350 degree oven, or until done. Cool before slicing.

INDEX